Small Habits
Revolution

10 Steps To Transforming Your Life
Through The Power Of Mini Habits!

An ArtOfProductivity.com Action Guide

Damon Zahariades

Other Books by Damon Zahariades

Morning Makeover: How To Boost Your Productivity, Explode Your Energy, and Create An Extraordinary Life - One Morning At A Time!

If you win the morning, you win the day. Here's how to create a morning routine that can literally change your life!

* * *

Fast Focus: A Quick-Start Guide To Mastering Your Attention, Ignoring Distractions, And Getting More Done In Less Time!

Are you constantly distracted? Does your mind wander after just a few minutes? Learn how to develop laser-sharp focus!

* * *

To-Do List Formula: A Stress-Free Guide To Creating To-Do Lists That Work!

Finally! A step-by-step system for creating to-do lists that'll actually help you to get things done!

* * *

The 30-Day Productivity Plan: Break The 30 Bad Habits That Are Sabotaging Your Time Management - One Day At A Time!

Need a daily action plan to boost your productivity? This 30-day guide is the solution to your time management woes!

* * *

The Time Chunking Method: A 10-Step Action Plan For Increasing Your Productivity

It's one of the most popular time management strategies used today. Double your productivity with this easy 10-step system.

* * *

Digital Detox: Unplug To Reclaim Your Life

Addicted to technology? Here's how to disconnect and enjoy real, meaningful connections that lead to long-term happiness.

* * *

Small Habits Revolution: 10 Steps To Transforming Your Life Through The Power Of Mini Habits!

Got 5 minutes a day? Use this simple, effective plan for creating any new habit you desire!

* * *

For a complete list, please visit
http://artofproductivity.com/my-books/

Your Free Gift

 I have a gift for you. It won't cost you a dime. It's a 40-page PDF guide titled *Catapult Your Productivity! The Top 10 Habits You Must Develop To Get More Things Done.* It's short enough to read quickly, but meaty enough to offer actionable advice to can change your life.

Claim your copy of *Catapult Your Productivity* at   the link below and join my mailing list:

http://artofproductivity.com/free-gift/

Before we dig into *Small Habits Revolution: 10 Steps To Transforming Your Life Through The Power Of Mini Habits!*, thanks are in order. I'd like to thank YOU. There are numerous books available that promise to show you how to develop good habits. You've chosen to read mine. For that, I'm grateful and honored.

On that note, let's roll up our sleeves and get our hands dirty. You're going to love what's coming your way in the following pages.

Contents

Foreword

I used to joke with my wife that we could train our dog to be a ninja assassin if we truly wanted. Dogs can be trained to do just about anything. The keys are repetition and consistency.

We're similar to dogs in that respect. We can train ourselves to the point that we're capable of accomplishing almost anything.

We can learn to speak new languages. We can learn to survive in the wilderness. We can learn to cook delicious, mouth-watering meals. We can learn to parallel park (no small feat for some of us!)

And we can train ourselves to adopt new, life-enriching habits that improve our long-term health, wealth, and productivity.

That's the purpose of this action guide. I'm going to show you the best method for creating positive, healthy habits. And importantly, I'm going to show you how to make these habits stick.

* * *

Our habits define us. They determine who we are, how we work, and whether we achieve our goals. They dictate how we interact with others and relate to the world around us. Creating good habits is thus important if we hope to lead healthy, happy, rewarding lives.

The problem is, good habits are difficult to form. And once we develop them, they're difficult to make stick. How many times have you promised yourself to start exercising only to let the habit slip after a few days? I can relate. I've done the same many times.

But suppose you knew a method for developing good habits that didn't make you feel as if you were fighting a tidal wave of resistance. Further suppose that method practically guaranteed your new habits persisted over the long run.

Imagine the healthy changes you could make in your life. Imagine the confidence you'd experience knowing that those healthy changes would endure regardless of the temptations.

Sound intriguing? If so, you're in the right place.

In this book, I'm going to share with you the proven 10-step strategy for creating good habits. This strategy will work for any behavioral pattern you can imagine. And the best part is, it'll all but ensure your newly-formed routines stick.

Before we dive into the good stuff, let's take a moment to discuss what this action guide *won't* cover. I think you'll be pleased.

What This Action Guide Will NOT Cover

Most books that address habit development fall into one of two categories.

The first category is made up of books that are heavy on science. They explain every aspect of the brain and how these aspects affect our ability to develop and sustain new habits. They talk about the amygdala, basil ganglia, various neurotransmitters, and the electrochemical processes that contribute to the rituals we perform.

The second category is made up of books that are little more than fluff. They completely ignore the science and focus on making the reader *feel* as if he or she can do anything. They're the written version of cheerleading. They offer little to no practical, actionable advice on habit development, but provide emotional validation in its stead.

Small Habits Revolution travels the road between these two categories.

First, we're not going to spend a lot of time on the science. Some aspects concerning how the brain works are worth mentioning as they relate to forming good habits. I'll highlight these aspects when doing so has practical value. But by and large, we're going to sidestep the branch of scientific knowledge that deals with the brain. While I find it fascinating, I believe its inclusion will only impede the discussion and hamper your success.

Second, we're not going to spend a lot of time on the cheerleading aspect. To be sure, I'm a firm believer in the power of encouragement, and you'll find plenty of it throughout *Small Habits Revolution*. But we're going to go much further. This action guide is designed for practical application. I'm going to show you the proven, step-by-step method for making healthy, lasting changes in your life. I've used it myself (and continue to do so today), as have millions of other people.

Third, *Small Habits Revolution* focuses on building good habits. To that end, we're not going to cover how to break bad habits. Curbing unhealthy routines is an entirely different topic and deserves its own book. Even the process of replacing bad habits with good ones is beyond the scope of this action guide.

In these pages, we're going to concentrate on one theme: how to build healthy habits that last the test of time.

Up next, you'll get a bird's-eye view of what's coming your way in *Small Habits Revolution*.

What You'll Learn In
Small Habits Revolution

Small Habits Revolution is comprised of seven fast-moving sections. Each one is a vital part of the discussion. Each one will prove to be crucial in helping you to form good habits that stick.

Having said that, I've organized the material in a way that allows you to easily jump to whichever section you desire at any time. You'll notice the table of contents is rich with detail. It'll make navigating this action guide a snap if you decide to jump from section to section.

Here's a quick breakdown of what each of the seven sections covers:

Part I

It's important to recognize what you stand to gain from building good habits. Part I highlights the benefits you'll enjoy, both now and in the future, as you make positive changes in your life.

This section will inspire you to take action. It'll also encourage you to move forward when you stumble. You may find yourself revisiting Part I for this purpose as you adopt new habits that set the stage for a more rewarding lifestyle.

Part II

It's also important to recognize how our minds adopt new habits. We'll delve into this topic in Part II. We'll talk about the concept of triggers and how to use them to make habits stick. We'll also discuss how routines are developed as well as the value of rewards.

As I mentioned earlier, we're going to avoid the heavy science. Instead, we'll focus on the practical aspects of the mind that are immediately applicable to making positive, lasting changes.

Part III

You've probably thought at some point that you just need the right motivation to form a particular habit (for example, going to the gym). Or you might believe that sticking to good habits is solely a matter of willpower.

In Part III, I'll explain why neither motivation nor willpower are critical to building positive behaviors in your life. This is good news if you're having difficulty sustaining either of them. I'll instead highlight the most important aspect of new habit development, and demonstrate how it's in your control.

Part IV

Part IV of *Small Habits Revolution* provides a simple 10-step plan for adopting a new routine into your life. This strategy will work for any habit you wish to develop. It's just a matter of following the plan.

I'll explain each step and explain why it's important to the habit development process. I'll also share actionable tips - things you can start doing immediately - to adopt the positive changes that will improve your life.

Part V

Unfortunately, having the best habit development strategy in place doesn't, by itself, guarantee your success. Much will depend on your process. Part V addresses this topic with more actionable advice.

This section of the book provides you with seven guidelines for adopting new routines. Each one is simple, but can make the difference between starting a habit that sticks and starting one that falls by the wayside.

In my opinion, Part V is just as important as Part IV, where I show you the simple 10-step plan for developing new habits. You'll find they go hand in hand.

Part VI

The most difficult part of developing new habits is making them last. It's easy to let ourselves slip. For example, according to Statistic Brain, only 8% of U.S. adults follow through on their New Year's resolutions.

I wrote Part VI to help you be the exception to the rule. This section of *Small Habits Revolution* will show you how to make new habits stick for the long run. As in previous sections, I'll provide actionable tips, including a simple, effective system used by the comedian Seinfeld (I use it myself).

Part VII

You may be at a loss regarding the types of small, positive habits you should adopt in your life. Part VII will help jumpstart your creative juices by providing nearly two dozen ideas.

The purpose of this section isn't to convince you to pursue a particular habit. As I've mentioned in my other action guides, you're the captain of your ship. You choose your own path. My goal is this section is to give you a springboard from which you can brainstorm new ways to improve your lifestyle.

* * *

Now that you know what to expect in the pages that follow, let me remind you that you're in control. I encourage you to read *Small Habits Revolution* front to back if this is your first time. Later, return to sections that offer you the greatest value according to wherever you are in the habit development process.

Part I

How Developing Healthy Habits Improves Your Quality Of Life

You wouldn't bother trying to adopt new habits unless there were a benefit to doing so. That's true for anything we pursue in life. We act with *purpose*.

The fact is, there are *many* rewards and benefits for developing positive behavioral patterns. You'll learn about them in this section. By the time you finish reading Part I, you'll have a clear glimpse of the lifestyle you can lead when you build good habits.

Let's begin by talking about your stress levels...

Lower Stress Levels

Stress isn't necessarily bad. It's what triggers our fight-or-flight response, which is designed to protect us from harm in certain circumstances. Small, short-term bouts of stress can literally save our lives.

Stress becomes a problem when it persists for extended periods. It manifests in a number of unpleasant ways.

It affects the way we treat people. If you're like me, you become irritable when you're stressed out.

It also causes physical side effects, such as headaches, heartburn, stomach problems, and even back pain. Ever felt achy when circumstances at the office or at home are chaotic? Stress is likely a contributor.

Long periods of high stress can also make you feel depressed, prevent you from sleeping, and impair your immune system. And if your immune system isn't working properly, you'll be more susceptible to sickness.

There are a myriad of ways to cope with stress, from doing yoga and practicing deep breathing to drinking tea and listening to soft music. The problem is, most people perform these activities as one-time affairs or on an as-needed basis.

There's a better approach: identify activities that make you feel better (i.e. less stressed) and make them daily *habits*.

For example, suppose you feel overwhelmed by your responsibilities at the office. Do a few pushups, sit-ups, and squats, and note how they make you feel. You'll probably feel more "alive." This is the result of endorphins kicking in, reducing your stress and improving your mood.

Take the simple act of drinking a glass of water when you wake up in the morning. That single habit ensures you're hydrated, which keeps your cortisol levels in check. (Cortisol is a stress hormone.)

Adopting good habits can dramatically reduce your stress levels. And when you're less stressed, you'll feel better, treat your loved ones better, and have a better outlook on life.

That's something we should all aim for!

Better Focus

Most of us would love to improve our ability to concentrate. A lack of concentration impacts our performance at school and at our jobs. It also negatively affects the relationships we share with our friends and loved ones.

If you're a student, and find it difficult to focus, you may be forced to burn the midnight oil completing assignments and studying for tests. If you're a corporate manager, it might mean staying late to finish tasks that should have been completed earlier in the day. An inability to focus will also make it more difficult to pay attention to your spouse, kids, and friends when they talk to you.

There are lots of exercises you can do to improve your concentration. For example, you can practice memorization routines. But you can also develop your ability to focus naturally by adopting certain habits.

For example, suppose one of the changes you'd like to make is to read more. You're tired of the snippets of information found on Google. You've grown weary of our sound bite culture, which presents news in tiny fragments masquerading as substantive content.

So you commit to reading books or long, informative articles each day. The act of doing so will improve your concentration. You'll be training your mind to focus on a single article or book rather than being distracted by the endless stream of fragmented content found online.

You can also develop the habit of attentive listening. Here, you would consciously spend time each day being present when talking to someone. You'd focus on what he or she is saying to the exclusion of everything else around you. This single habit will improve your ability to concentrate. As a bonus, it'll also communicate to your friends and loved ones that they're important to you.

Good habits set the stage for better focus. And better focus leads to improved performance, stronger relationships, and a boost in productivity.

Improved Productivity

In the last section, I noted that improving your focus will increase your productivity. You know this from experience. Recall the last time you worked in a flow state, where the entirety of your attention was devoted to the task in front of you. You probably found it easy to work without distractions, and were able to efficiently complete the task.

That's one example of how good habits lead to greater productivity. Here's another: suppose you develop the habit of waking up an hour earlier each day. Can you imagine how this new routine might affect your productivity? You'll likely be able to get more done in less time.

Or suppose you develop the habit of cleaning your desk at the end of each workday. Or checking email twice a day rather than 20 times a day. Or taking regular breaks so that your brain has a chance to rest. Or setting realistic deadlines for tasks.

You get the idea. These small habits, all of them easy to develop and maintain with my 10-step strategy, will help you to ignore distractions and get more done.

The result? You'll have more free time to spend with your family and friends. You'll have more time to devote to your hobbies and passions. You'll also enjoy more energy, less stress, and better relationships.

The best part is that the boost in your productivity occurs naturally as a result of your new habits. You can focus on developing new, healthy lifestyle routines without having to devote attention specifically to increasing your productivity. The latter happens as a natural extension of the former.

This is a compelling benefit to look forward to!

Stronger Relationships

The relationships we share with our friends and loved ones determine our overall happiness. The strength of those relationships is influenced by our ability and willingness to form sincere connections.

Think about the types of positive habits that support this effort. For example, I mentioned earlier that listening attentively to someone - that is, *focusing* your attention on him or her - will make the individual feel valued by you. This feeling opens the door to a deeper level of trust and intimacy.

Likewise, consider the positive effect of giving your spouse a sincere hug and kiss each morning before you head to the office. It's a small display of affection. But these days, with shows of affection a common casualty of our ever-busy schedules, this small display can have a monumental effect on the emotional closeness you share with your spouse.

These are merely a couple of examples demonstrating how positive routines (one-time actions made into habits) can improve your relationships. Here are a few other ideas:

- Schedule 30 minutes of one-on-one time with your spouse each day (no television, no kids, no phones, etc.). Use the time to talk without distractions.
- Give your spouse a daily compliment.
- Call or visit your parents once a week.

- Be encouraging and supportive when your friends share their thoughts with you.
- Tell the truth when asked for your opinion. Friends will appreciate your candor and trust your sincerity.

These small habits improve the closeness of your relationships. They foster trust and encourage a deeper sense of connectedness. Such bonds are more likely to last the test of time than the ones saddled by poor listening and inattentiveness.

Greater Sense Of Joy

When we establish and maintain positive, healthy habits, we experience a more rewarding lifestyle. For example, consider how low stress levels, improved concentration, a boost in productivity, and stronger relationships might influence your quality of life. You'll feel more relaxed, get more done in less time, and enjoy more sincere, intimate bonds with your friends and loved ones.

Of course, these benefits are just the tip of the iceberg. There are many more, which we'll discuss in detail in a few moments. The point is, adopting positive behaviors sets the stage for living an enriching life.

Think of the myriad ways in which healthy routines can improve your daily experience. You can enjoy better physical and mental health. You can feel more energized and confident. You can develop previously-unimagined levels of grit and self-discipline.

To a large extent, your habits and routines also dictate your accomplishments. Some will make it easier to learn new concepts, develop new skills, and think more creatively. Others focus on physical fitness, and can help you to lose weight, get into shape, and feel better.

You probably have a list of things you hope to achieve - at home and in your career, in the present and down the road. Leaving them to happenstance is a surefire recipe for failure.

Instead, create positive routines that support your goals.

Once these routines become a part of your life, to the point you no longer think about doing them (i.e. they become automatic), they'll fill you with a sense of well-being. A sense of joy. They'll improve your mood and outlook on life. They'll also help you to feel great about yourself as you gain more control over your responses to personal and environmental triggers.

Better Sleep Quality

If you knew there was an easy way to be more creative, feel more energized, and experience fewer mood swings, would you pursue it? What if you could enjoy healthier skin, greater focus, and make fewer mistakes during the course of your day? And what if, in the bargain, you were less likely to get sick and more likely to feel better each day?

This is starting to sound like an informercial.

The fact is, these are all documented effects of getting a good night's sleep. Experts have long known that the quality of our sleep dictates how we feel and how we perform.

If you're a student, it affects your ability to study and do well on tests.

If you're an entrepreneur, it influences how you make business decisions.

If you're a corporate manager, if affects how you relate to the people on your team.

If you're a stay-at-home parent, it shapes how you interact with your children.

The good news is that developing positive routines can help improve the quality of your sleep. For example, suppose you get into the habit of doing one or more of the following:

- Go to bed an hour earlier each night
- Turn off your television an hour before going to bed

- Avoid caffeine six hours before going to sleep
- Listen to your favorite piano sonata before bedtime
- Go to bed at the same time each night

Once these habits become a part of your nightly routine, you'll find it easier to fall asleep. Moreover, you'll be more likely to enjoy *restful, uninterrupted* sleep. Do these things night after night, and you'll feel more rested and energized, less stressed and agitated, and healthier and happier when you're awake.

That's the power of incorporating small, positive routines in your life.

Improved Physical Health

Good physical health is something we should all strive for. Good health helps us to live more rewarding lives. Staying in shape allows us to more easily control our weight and enjoy better-quality sleep. And of course, it also makes us less susceptible to heart problems, metabolic syndrome, and diabetes.

When most people think about what it takes to stay in shape, they instinctively think of their diet and exercise regimen. Good health is associated with eating healthy foods (and avoiding unhealthy ones) and exercising on a regular basis.

The problem is, doing these things is difficult. Most of us face a high degree of internal resistance. For example, we crave ice cream and chips, making it tough to stick to a healthy diet. And we'd rather binge-watch the latest season of *The Walking Dead* or *House of Cards* than grab our shoes and head to the gym.

But what if you could improve your physical health by developing tiny habits that take little time or effort? Here are few examples:

- Do five pushups per day
- Do five squats per day
- Go for a 10-minute walk
- Drink a glass of water when you wake up
- Reduce meal portions by 10%

Notice how none of the above habits are difficult to do. Nor do they take a lot of time. You can do five pushup in less than 30 seconds. You can perform five squats just as quickly. But you'll find that if you do them day after day, your physical health will only improve.

One of my first experiences with small habits came in the form of doing pushups. It opened my eyes to the effectiveness of starting small.

I had tried to start exercising many times in the past. I tried to compel myself to go to the gym, start doing pushups and sit-ups, and even start jogging.

Of course, it never happened. The thought of doing these things was too daunting.

So I made a commitment. I'd do five pushups a day. No more, no less. I started this new regimen that day.

During the first week, that's all I did. Five pushups a day. The following week, I bumped the number to six. The week after that, I increased it to seven. And so forth.

Today, I do 25 pushups per day. I've created a recurring to-do item in Todoist as a daily reminder. But frankly, I don't need it. Doing the 25 pushups is now like brushing my teeth. It has become an ingrained habit. I don't feel right unless I've done them.

I may not (yet) have the body of Adonis, but I can definitely tell the difference between now and when I first started. I look better and feel better. It's all due to that first day, when I made the decision to do just five pushups.

Later in this action guide, I'll go into more detail regarding how I made this positive behavior a daily habit. You'll be surprised and delighted by the simplicity of my approach. I'm 100% confident it will work for you just as it has for me.

Ability To Make
Lightning-Fast Decisions

General Patton once said, "*A good plan violently executed now is better than a perfect plan next week.*" I've found this to be true in nearly all circumstances.

But making fast decisions didn't come naturally to me. I used to overthink everything. Consequently, it took me forever to make decisions in my personal and professional lives.

The downside was that I missed out on countless opportunities. It affected my relationships with friends and loved ones. It hampered my ability to do my job efficiently when I was trapped in Corporate America. It hurt my productivity as an entrepreneur.

I eventually learned to make quick decisions. It was a long process. I had to first commit to making the change and then develop new behaviors to support it.

Here's what I did to get comfortable with making fast decisions:

- I gave myself 60 seconds to make a decision when no additional information was needed.
- When additional information *was* needed, I set a time limit to acquire it (e.g. five minutes).
- I gave myself permission to make bad decisions.
- I trained myself to ask "*Am I overthinking this?*"

whenever I hesitated.

- When presented with multiple options, I immediately eliminated the 80% that made the least sense.
- Like most people, I'm averse to failure. So I trained myself to embrace it, if only as constructive feedback.

By developing these six small habits, I was able to dramatically lessen the time I required to make decisions. I'm glad I made the effort. I've not only found that making fast decisions leads to more opportunities, but *bad* decisions seldom have severe consequences. In my experience, overthinking things yields little practical value.

I'm willing to bet you'll find this to be true in your own life. If you tend to overanalyze things, adopt the small routines I described above. You'll be floored by how easily you can go from over-thinker to speedy decision-maker with the help of a few small, easy-to-perform habits.

Increased Creativity

Our lives are so busy and we're so encumbered by our responsibilities at home and at the office that being creative can seem self-indulgent. But experts say creativity leads to greater innovation, better problem-solving skills, less stress, and improved mood.

That being the case, it's worth striving to become more creative.

You probably know someone who claims he or she isn't creative. But that was true for all of us at some point. Creativity is like a muscle. It's learned. In fact, more colleges than ever are now offering classes that teach students how to be creative.

But you don't need to attend college to build this muscle. You can do it on your own with the help of a few small habits.

For example, commit to digging deeply into topics of interest. Most of us neglect to do that. We've become accustomed to relying on Google for information. We perform a few search queries, find the details we need, and move on. We don't do the "deep dive" into the material that leads to creative thought.

Digging into details opens up the mind and often reveals ideas that may not have surfaced otherwise.

The best part is that this is an easy habit to adopt. It's just a matter of doing it with consistency.

Another small, simple habit that can strengthen your creativity muscle is daydreaming. Letting your mind wander allows your brain to make associations it might otherwise miss.

It introduces strange thoughts and ideas that are normally suppressed while performing boring tasks. Unsurprisingly, studies have shown that daydreaming helps individuals brainstorm innovative solutions to tough problems.

The point is that you can learn to be more creative and enjoy the benefits of greater creativity. All it takes is adopting a few tiny habits.

Greater Self-Confidence

Self-confidence is an elusive trait for many people. It's also frustrating since some folks make it seem so easy. These extroverted individuals, often the life of the party, seem to have been born with a special self-assuredness gene.

But as with most traits, self-confidence can be learned. You can train yourself to greet people with enthusiasm, maintain eye contact, and radiate a sense of zest that draws people to you.

How do you get to the point where your belief in yourself encourages others to believe in you? How do you learn to trust your instincts and make decisions with assertiveness and authority? In short, how do you develop confidence?

You don't have to take an expensive course. Nor do you need to spend hours in front of a mirror practicing how you speak. Growth in self-confidence can result from developing a few simple habits. Here are several ideas:

- Practice maintaining eye contact with baristas at Starbucks, the clerks at your local grocery store, and strangers you meet while waiting in line.
- Upgrade your attire.
- Say hello to one stranger each day.
- Smile whenever you establish eye contact.
- Identify a small problem and solve it.

- Whenever you doubt your abilities, whether to solve a problem, complete a task, or hold a conversation, ask yourself why. In most cases, the reason is emotional rather than logical.

That's just scratching the surface, of course. But notice that none of the habits above are difficult to develop and maintain. All of them are tiny actions you can take starting today. That's the main theme of *Small Habits Revolution*: start small so it's easy to get started right away.

You may feel uncomfortable in the beginning - for example, if you're unaccustomed to looking people in the eye - but that's the case with learning any new behavior. The good news is that it becomes easier with practice.

Here's the takeaway: adopting small, healthy routines - importantly, ones that take very little time or effort to perform - can lead to major growth in your self-confidence over time.

Stronger Commitment To Your Goals

It feels great to achieve our goals. Doing so fills us with a gratifying sense of accomplishment. Achieving our goals gives us confidence that we can achieve others, and the impetus to act on them.

For example, think back to the last time you took steps to lose a few pounds. Didn't it feel great when you looked at the scale and realized you had met your goal?

Or maybe you wanted to learn how to play the piano. Can you recall the sense of accomplishment you felt after becoming proficient?

We set goals to improve our lives. This might entail losing weight, getting into shape, learning a new skill, or investing for the future. Most of us are inspired to strive for a better, more rewarding lifestyle.

The challenge is remaining *committed* to our goals. It's one thing to set them. It's another thing entirely to stay motivated enough to pursue them day after day. This is the reason so many people abandon their goals. They see little improvement and few benefits in the short run, which discourages them from pushing forward.

For example, consider the intention to lose 25 pounds. Most health experts suggest losing weight slowly, to the tune of two pounds per week. At that rate, it would take the individual nearly three months to achieve his or her goal. That's a long time to wait for goal fulfillment. It's understandable that such an individual might abandon the goal for something that leads to quicker gratification.

There's a much better approach. Consistent with the theme of *Small Habits Revolution*, it involves adopting small, easy-to-perform routines that lead to big results. Developing and maintaining simple daily routines shifts the focus from the struggle to accomplish the end goal. It removes the biggest source of discouragement, making goal abandonment less likely. Instead, the focus is placed on maintaining healthy habits, which, with time, ultimately lead to goal fulfillment.

For example, the person who wants to lose 25 pounds would ignore what the scale says each night. Instead, he or she would focus on maintaining the following habits:

- Drink a glass of water after waking up each morning.
- Only shop the perimeter of a grocery store, where the healthy foods are displayed. (Junk food is usually found in the center aisles.)
- Reduce meal sizes by 10%.
- Chew food slowly and savor the taste.
- Eat breakfast.
- Take a 10-minute walk each day. Twice a day is better.
- Eat three meals a day at consistent times (e.g. breakfast at 7:00 a.m., lunch at noon, dinner at 6:00 p.m.)
- Snack on healthy, filling foods. Examples include almonds, apples, and carrots with hummus.

Maintaining the above habits will help the person who wants to lose weight to do so. Notice that the focus is no longer on the number of pounds lost. Instead, small, healthy, easy-to-implement routines are the star of the show.

Bottom line: it's easier to remain committed to your goals when you focus on the small habits that lead to them rather than the goals themselves.

Part II

Triggers, Routines, Rewards, And Loops

Every habit, good or bad, healthy or unhealthy, is prompted by a trigger. When the habit is performed, it is either rewarded or punished. When habits are rewarded, they become behavioral loops, which reinforce themselves over time.

It's important to understand how this works.

I noted earlier that we're going to avoid the heavy brain science in *Small Habits Revolution*. As fascinating as the brain is, spending a lot of time digging into cognitive psychology offers limited practical value. You're reading this action guide to improve your life. That being the case, we're going to focus on actionable strategies.

Having said that, it's impossible to enjoy real, lasting success in adopting new habits without having at least a nominal understanding concerning how these habits develop and stick.

This section of *Small Habits Revolution* deals with triggers, routine, rewards, and loops. We're going to move quickly. So grab a glass of water, settle in, and hold on tight.

First Things First: Definitions

I'm going to introduce a number of terms you may be unfamiliar with. It's important to understand them in the context of habit development. (Credit to Charles Duhigg for discussing them in his book *The Power of Habit.*)

Let's start with the four terms I mentioned at the beginning of Part II.

Trigger

A trigger is the cue or circumstance that spurs you to perform an action. For example, suppose you're inclined to eat ice cream when you're bored. Boredom is the trigger for your ice cream habit.

Routine

A routine is an action performed over and over. It's another way of referring to a habit or behavioral pattern.

We tend to think of routines as single actions. But they're actually composed of series of actions. Consider the habit of eating ice cream as an example. Here's the sequence: you stop what you're doing (first action), get up from your chair (second action), walk to your freezer (third action), fix yourself a bowl of ice cream (fourth action), and sit down to enjoy it (fifth action).

Breaking things down in this manner may seem pedestrian. But it reveals what's involved in developing a new routine and making it stick. Each action in the series is a potential snare where the routine can collapse. This is the reason starting small, the core theme of *Small Habits Revolution*, is such an effective strategy. It streamlines the habit development process, thereby minimizing the impact of potential roadblocks.

Reward

Rewards reinforce routines. They represent what you gain whenever you perform an action or series of actions.

In our ice cream example, the reward may be the treat's sweet taste and creamy texture. Or it may be the feeling of contentment that results from the massive dopamine release triggered by sugar consumption.

Understanding the reasons we perform specific routines begins with identifying the rewards that encourage them.

Loop

A loop encompasses the three ideas above. Every behavioral loop consists of a trigger, a routine, and a reward.

This is a key concept to understand. It shows that habits develop and stick as the result of stimuli. That's good news since we can control the stimuli to which we expose ourselves. We thus have the ability to develop any new routine we desire. It's just a matter of setting up the proper conditions. As you'll see in the following pages, this is easier than you may think.

Keystone Habit

A keystone habit is a routine that influences, and even triggers, other routines or behaviors.

For example, suppose you've adopted the time chunking method as a productivity strategy in your workday. You've found that when you use time chunks, you're able to focus on your work. You're less likely to waste time on Facebook, CNN, and YouTube. You're also less likely to text your friends, play video games, and amuse yourself with your phone's apps. In this case, your use of the time chunking method is a keystone habit.

Keystone habits can - and should - be leveraged to develop new routines. For example, if you start exercising each day, you may be more inclined to eat healthy food. If you wake up an hour earlier each morning, you might find it easier to drink more water, starting with the first glass upon waking. One habit influences the other.

These five definitions will help to clarify the ideas found throughout the rest of this action guide. They'll prove invaluable when we get to my simple 10-step plan for developing new habits that stick.

Let's now explore the five different types of triggers.

The Five Different Types Of Triggers

Triggers are arguably the most important part of the habit puzzle. They dictate what we do and when we do it. They also influence the extent to which a habit is reinforced in our minds. Consistent application of routines, the key to making them last, owe a lot to the cues that prompt us to act.

In this section, we're going to discuss the five types of triggers. Understanding how they work is invaluable. Once you understand them, you'll be able to put them to use in developing and maintaining any habit you believe will enrich your life.

Let's start with the trigger that everyone is familiar with, even if they don't recognize it outright.

Time

Most of us go through certain routines based on what time it is. For example, when I wake up at 5:30 a.m., I brush my teeth, wash my face, use the restroom, drink a glass of water, and get dressed. At 1:00 p.m., I eat lunch. Around 6:00 p.m., I eat dinner. Immediately before going to bed, I brush my teeth again.

I'm sure you follow similar patterns. Perhaps you have a cup of coffee when you wake up. Maybe you enjoy a cigarette break each day at 10:30 a.m. Or you might savor a glass of pinot noir each evening at 9:00 p.m.

Time is one of the most common cues. It's a valuable tool for developing new routines because it's easy to control.

Location

Many habits are triggered based on setting. For example, most of us associate our kitchens with food preparation. When we visit this part of our homes, our brains are already primed to act according to that directive. Many of us thus instinctively veer toward our refrigerators to look for food.

Think about the location-based cues you act upon. Do you grab a cup of coffee the moment you arrive at the office? Do you check your email the moment you arrive at school? Do you surf social media sites while sitting at Starbucks?

Just like time-based triggers, you can easily leverage location-based triggers to form new behavioral patterns. We'll talk about this in greater detail in the next section, titled *How Triggers And Routines Lead To New Habits.*

State Of Mind

Our state of mind plays a major role in our behaviors. How we *feel* influences how we *act.*

For example, many people eat when they experience a high level of stress. Many instinctively check Facebook and Twitter when they're bored. Some reach for their phones to call their friends when they feel cheerful. Some take naps when they feel depressed.

The point is, our emotions are a powerful trigger. They

prompt us to follow learned routines, healthy or unhealthy.

Psychologists claim we can control our state of mind. That's useful because it means we can tailor our emotional state so that it triggers healthy routines. All it takes is the willingness to anchor a desired habit to a particular emotion.

For example, suppose you want to get into the habit of taking short walks. Anchor the activity to boredom. Each time you feel bored, stand up and go for a 10-minute walk. Here, the emotion is used to cue the desired routine.

People

You've probably heard people describe themselves as social drinkers. They rarely drink at home, but regularly imbibe when they're with their friends. Their drinking habit is based on the people around them.

This type of behavioral response is common. The people with whom we associate are a potent trigger for many of our routines.

For example, you might smoke with certain people at the office during a morning break. You might be more inclined to exercise when you get together with your workout buddies. You may have an accountability partner who motivates you to get things done.

Whether we realize it or not, we train ourselves to respond in various ways to the people in our lives. That's good news. If you can associate, or anchor, a positive habit to someone in your life, you can use the association as a reliable trigger.

Preceding Event

As noted earlier, many (if not most) of our routines are comprised of a series of actions. One action follows the other. That action precedes another, which is followed by yet another, and so on.

To illustrate, think about the process you go through when getting ready for bed. You might take a shower, drink a glass of water, brush your teeth, and put on your pajamas. And if you're like me, you do these things in the same order each night. One action predictably precedes the next. There's little variance from night to night.

In the context of developing new habits, this behavior can be leveraged via a strategy known as "habit stacking." You form new habits by anchoring them to *current* habits.

For example, suppose you want to get into the habit of flossing your teeth. Anchor the activity to *brushing* your teeth, the logical preceding event. Reach for your floss immediately after you finish brushing, allowing the current habit to trigger the new habit.

You can use habit stacking in a myriad of ways to develop positive, healthy routines. We'll discuss it in more detail in *Part VI: How To Guarantee Your New Habits Will Last*. As you'll soon see, it's an ideal approach to developing small habits that grow and last the test of time.

How Triggers And Routines
Lead To New Habits

In the previous section, we covered the five different types of triggers (time, location, state of mind, people, and preceding events). We also discussed, albeit briefly, how these triggers can be used to create new behavioral patterns.

In this section, we're going to go into more detail. This topic is of the utmost importance because it impacts how successful you are in adopting new habits that stick.

As we noted earlier, every habit is preceded by a cue. For example, hunger triggers the impulse to eat. Sleepiness triggers the impulse to take a nap. For some, stress triggers the impulse to smoke or drink.

Technically, habits stem from routines. A stimulus (hunger, sleepiness, stress, etc.) prompts us to perform a routine, or a sequence of actions. These actions become habit when the routine becomes ingrained in our minds.

Here's a simple example. Suppose you watch the evening news each night, after which you go to bed. The end of the news program serves as the cue. It triggers a sequence of actions, such as brushing your teeth, putting on your pajamas, etc., that culminates with your climbing into bed and going to sleep.

By going through this routine night after night, it becomes deeply rooted in your mind. It eventually becomes a habit.

Consider what that means in terms of developing small,

positive habits that enhance your quality of life. If you can anchor a desired behavioral pattern to a particular cue, you can develop any habit you can imagine.

Let me give you an example of how I'm currently using this strategy.

As you know, I write books that offer step-by-step plans for being more productive and designing a more rewarding lifestyle. I also maintain a popular blog (artofproductivity.com).

As much as I enjoy writing, I'm not always motivated to do it. It's highly enjoyable and incredibly rewarding work, but it takes a considerable amount of focus and effort to do it well.

Up until a few years ago, I approached writing without the use of a dependable trigger. I relied on motivation and willpower - in Part III, you'll see why neither are sufficient for developing new habits - and consequently, my output was less than stellar.

Then I stumbled upon a piano piece by Chopin: Prelude in E Minor Op. 28, No. 4. It changed everything. I found it to be simultaneously magical and hypnotic. I quickly discovered that I could reach a flow state while writing as the piece played in the background.

I decided to use the Chopin piece as a cue. Whenever I intended to write, I put in my earbuds and played Prelude in E Minor Op. 28, No. 4 in the background. I set it to play on a loop. Without fail, my mind instantly went into writing mode.

I do a significant amount of writing in coffeeshops, such as Starbucks. The downside of working in these types of places is that it's tempting to people watch rather than write. I could waste hours observing people and consequently get nothing done.

Here's where the Chopin piece has been invaluable for helping me to maintain focus and build my writing habit. Whenever I sit down at a table, whether it's at Starbucks, It's A Grind, or Panera Bread, the first thing I do is put in my earbuds. I queue Prelude in E Minor Op. 28, No. 4 and order my drink (a Caffè Americano, if you're curious). By the time I sit down, my mind is already in writing mode.

The Chopin piece is my trigger. It helps me to focus. Most importantly, it reinforces my writing habit.

Would I be inclined to write at Starbucks *without* listening Prelude in E Minor Op. 28, No. 4? Maybe. But this trigger works so well for me in this context that there's no reason for me not to use it.

Think about triggers *you* can use to develop new routines that turn into long-term habits. It's a near certainty you're already doing numerous things that fit the bill. Once you identify those that can serve as effective cues, anchor your desired habits to them.

Now that we've talked about triggers, let's talk about rewards - specifically, how they reinforce our behavioral patterns.

How Rewards Reinforce Newly-Formed Habits

You're already familiar with the use of rewards as a form of positive reinforcement for desired behaviors. We use them all the time. For example, we use treats to encourage our dogs to behave or perform tricks. We use assorted incentives to encourage our children to get good grades in school. We offer bonuses to our employees to motivate them to attain specific goals.

The same tactic will help you to adopt new, healthy habits.

Rewards are a part of every behavioral loop. It's safe to say that every action we take is motivated by some type of reward, whether we realize it or not. We exercise to look better. We eat to sate our hunger. We watch television to relax. We attend college to obtain a degree. We get a job to earn income.

Everything we do, from brushing our teeth to planning a week-long family vacation, is motivated by something we desire. In the short run, this desire involves satisfying a craving (e.g. we eat because we're hungry). In the long run, it involves achieving a specific goal (e.g. we obtain a college degree to work in our field of interest).

This is important to understand in the context of habit development because it gives us control. We can choose rewards that are important to us, and anchor our new behavioral patterns to them. We get the rewards as long as we maintain the patterns.

The key to making this work is to choose rewards that offer swift gratification.

For example, suppose you want to start exercising on a regular basis. Getting started is easy. If you've ever visited the gym during the first week of January, you'll see evidence of this. Keeping up the habit, however, is more difficult. You need a reward that prompts you to take action on a daily basis.

The thought of being in shape appeals to most people. But it's not a good reward in the context of developing the exercise habit. Why? Because it can take months to get into shape.

You need something that offers immediate gratification.

Suppose you have a favorite television program. Allow yourself to watch it if and only if you work out that day. Or suppose you love to take naps (if so, you're a person after my own heart). Allow yourself a 30-minute nap as a reward for exercising.

By anchoring the new habit to a swift and desirable reward, you signal to your brain that the habit is worth doing.

Not every reward will be effective for a given habit. You may need to test several to identify the one that has the greatest impact.

For example, let's say that while you enjoy taking naps, a 30-minute nap isn't enough of an inducement to spur you to exercise each day. In this case, you would test a different reward and note whether it has a bigger influence on you. Suppose you enjoy going to happy hour each afternoon with your coworkers. Conduct a test. Allow yourself to attend happy hour if and only if you exercise in the morning or during your lunch break. You may find that *this* reward does the trick.

Once you find a reward that motivates you to take action on a regular basis, use it until it loses its effectiveness. Be consistent. Although the routine is in place, the habit hasn't yet been developed. Habits develop through repetition.

Eventually, you won't need the reward to prompt you to take action. The habit will have become ingrained to the point that you do it without the need for immediate gratification. In fact, depending on the routine, you may start doing it without even thinking about it.

How To Create Strong Habit Loops

Thus far, we've covered triggers, routines, and rewards, and discussed how each plays an important role in developing new behaviors. Let's now talk about how they work together as a system.

These elements comprise a simple 3-step loop. The first step is a cue. The cue triggers a routine, the second step. Performing the routine results in a reward, the third and final step.

The reward at the end of the loop satisfies a craving and delivers a feeling of gratification.

Your brain remembers this process and stores it for future reference. At the first recognized opportunity, it'll seek to repeat the process in order to recreate the positive feeling. When the previously identified cue resurfaces, your brain will prompt you to once again perform the routine.

Think about how this natural, cognitive process can help you to create new, healthy habits that last.

In the section *How Triggers And Routines Lead To New Habits*, we noted that you have the ability to choose your own cues. Recall my personal example of using Chopin's Prelude in E Minor Op. 28, No. 4 as a cue to start writing.

In the section titled *How Rewards Reinforce Newly-Formed Habits*, we noted that you have the ability to choose your own rewards.

And of course, you get to select the habits you wish to make a part of your life.

In other words, you control every aspect of the habit development loop. That means you hold the key to your own success.

Let's use an example to drive this point home. Suppose you want to get into the habit of reading from a non-fiction book each night. You need to identify a cue and a reward.

Let's say you choose the end of the evening news as your cue. As soon as the program ends, you turn off your television and pick up your book. In keeping with the theme of *Small Habits Revolution*, you start small. You read for five minutes.

After you finish reading, you treat yourself to a glass of pinot noir, your favorite wine. That's your reward for performing the routine.

If you go through this process each night, the routine will eventually become a habit. You'll find yourself looking forward to reading non-fiction each night. With time, you'll need neither the cue to prompt the behavior nor the reward to serve as motivation. The habit will have become ingrained in your mind.

Remember, You're In Control

The most important thing to take away from this section of *Small Habits Revolution* is that you're in complete control. You control the entire habit loop. You dictate the extent to which you adopt and maintain new, positive habits in your life.

That's exciting news!

You don't have to rely on anybody else for success. Nor do you have to contend with circumstances that are outside your control. You create your own circumstances. As long as you can identify the right cues and rewards, you can develop any habit imaginable.

Be prepared to experiment to find what works best for you. The upside is that you can start building new, positive routines that enrich your life whenever you're ready.

In Part III, we're going to talk about motivation and willpower, and how they affect habit development. The facts may surprise you.

Part III

Motivation Vs. Willpower: Which One Dictates Your Success?

When we think of developing good habits, we instinctively assume that doing so takes motivation and willpower. We think we need something big to inspire us in the moment and spur us to take action. And once we take action, we reason that making good habits stick is a matter of determination.

That's what most of us were raised to believe.

But what if our assumptions about habit development are completely wrong? What if we've been misled about the roles of motivation and willpower in forming new routines? What if *neither* are keys to success?

That would explain why so many people, including those who are motivated and determined, fail to make good habits stick.

Part III of *Small Habits Revolution* will explore the dual roles of motivation and willpower. You'll discover why neither will match the effectiveness of a small habit that takes root and grows slowly with time.

Why Motivation Isn't Enough

"I'm unmotivated."

How many times have you heard that response when you ask people why they failed to take action? It's as if our ability to act is completely dependent on whether we're inspired to do so.

The right motivation can indeed spur us to action. For example, even if we're unabashed couch potatoes, we'll be motivated to run if a lion is chasing us.

The problem with motivation is that it's always short-lived. It never lasts. This means it's a terribly ineffective tool for developing new habits and making them stick. In fact, a growing body of scientific evidence suggests that the items that motivate us to take action can have the opposite effect once we do so.

Take the use of rewards as an example. As you know, rewards can be a powerful motivator. But psychologists have found that they can actually *demotivate* us. A study published in the Journal of Personality and Social Psychology in 1973 examined the effects of various rewards on children encouraged to draw. The authors found that when a reward was expected, the children spent *less* time drawing rather than more.

Other studies have revealed similar results. An analysis of 92 studies examining the effects of monetary rewards on job performance found there was virtually no correlation between the two elements. (The findings were reported in the Journal of Vocational Behavior in 2010.)

Why doesn't motivation work as a dependable prompt for consistent action? There are a few reasons.

First, it's inconstant. It ebbs and flows. BJ Fogg, founder of the Stanford Persuasive Technology Lab, refers to this effect as a "motivation wave." Your motivation levels rise and fall, which makes it an unreliable tool for designing new behaviors.

A second reason is that it's unpredictable. There's no way to anticipate when you'll feel motivated and when you'll feel unmotivated. That being the case, you can't rely on motivation to spur you to take action (i.e. perform your desired habit).

Third, as I mentioned above, motivation is short-lived. Although it's valuable for encouraging immediate action, it offers little encouragement for *repeated* action. Most of us experience motivation as a surge of excitement. It happens over a short period of time. We rarely, if ever, experience that same feeling day after day.

Fourth, motivation is often dependent on our internal messaging. For example, suppose your boss asks you to do something that doesn't feel right to you. It's difficult to get motivated if the deed is inconsistent with your values and beliefs.

Or suppose you've gotten into the habit of telling yourself you "have to" exercise. What's the first thing that surfaces whenever you feel you have to do anything?

Internal resistance.

Resistance is the nemesis of motivation. The two are like oil and water. They can't occupy the same space. When resistance rears its head, motivation tends to evaporate. You can hardly rely on it to help you develop new behavioral patterns, which require consistent action over time.

These are the reasons motivation will never be enough for creating and maintaining new, healthy routines. It can spur us to do unpleasant things, such as doing our taxes or visiting the dentist. But it's an ineffective tool for inspiring daily action.

If motivation isn't the answer, what about willpower? Does it offer the solution for creating habits that last? Let's find out in the next section.

Is Willpower The Solution?

If motivation inspires us to take action (albeit sporadically and unreliably), what spurs us to do so over and over?

Many people claim the answer is willpower. They assert that with enough determination and grit, we can make ourselves do things we would otherwise not do.

This is true to an extent. If we're committed to producing a certain outcome, we can force ourselves to act in order to effect that outcome. For example, suppose you're determined to jog one mile for exercise. You may have sufficient willpower to make yourself put on your running shoes and hit the track.

The question is, will you have enough willpower to do so tomorrow, the next day, and the next? Can you rely on personal determination to create and maintain this new habit?

The answer is no. There are two reasons.

First, scientists have discovered that willpower is a finite resource. It depletes over time. We'll discuss this idea further in the next section, titled *The Problem With Willpower*.

Second, willpower has a short-term nature. It's like a Roman candle; it burns brightly in the beginning, but quickly fizzles. This trait makes it a useful tool for resisting immediate temptations - for example, eating an ice cream sundae when you're on a diet. But it's less useful for developing new behavioral patterns, which require consistent application, ideally on a daily basis.

In the following section, we'll take a deeper dive into the

problems associated with willpower. You'll learn why determination alone isn't enough to create lasting routines. This is a crucial topic since so many people believe a lack of willpower is the reason they fail when they attempt to develop good habits.

The truth is much simpler. So is the solution.

But I'm getting ahead of myself. Let's first bury the notion once and for all that willpower is the key to creating positive, healthy habits.

The Problem With Willpower

In the previous section, I noted there were two big problems with willpower as a habit development tool. First, it's a finite resource. Second, its usefulness is limited to a short timeframe.

Let's talk about these two shortcomings in detail.

In 2011, the Proceedings of the National Academy of Sciences (PNAS) published a fascinating study. It was titled *Extraneous Factors In Judicial Decisions.* The authors sought to learn why judges' decisions tended to be favorable for prisoners in the morning, but less favorable as the day progressed. To introduce their study, they noted *"we test the common caricature of realism that justice is 'what the judge ate for breakfast.'"*

The authors examined more than 1,100 rulings over a period of 10 months. They found that the judges were more inclined to rule in favor of prisoners at the start of their workday and immediately following food breaks. But as the day wore on and the decision sessions lengthened, the judges became more inclined to render less favorable rulings in cases with similar legal circumstances.

The researchers chalked up the effect to "mental depletion." They opined the judges suffered from decision fatigue, which the data showed worsened with each ruling.

This study demonstrates the biggest shortcoming of willpower in the context of habit development: it's a finite resource. It's like a full tank of gas in your car. You start the day with a fixed store of willpower. But each decision you make consumes a part of it. By the end of the day, you have little to no willpower left, which makes it difficult to resist short-term temptations.

For example, suppose you want to get into the habit of jogging. If you commit to doing it as the first activity of each morning, you'll probably have the needed willpower. Assuming a good night's rest, you start the day with a "full tank of gas."

But what if you intend to go jogging after work? This can be problematic unless the habit is already a part of your daily schedule. By the time you arrive home from work, you'll have made hundreds of decisions during the course of your day. Each one will have consumed some of your willpower, leaving you with a severely-depleted supply.

As seen in the study examining judicial decisions, this depletion is the result of decision fatigue. You have minimal willpower "left in the tank" because you've used it up making decisions throughout the day. Consequently, you'll be more susceptible to short-term temptations. For example, you'll be more inclined to give in to the desire to relax on your couch and watch television instead of going jogging.

The fact that willpower is a finite resource that suffers depletion is a relatively recent discovery. But it poses far-reaching implications concerning its usefulness (or lack thereof) in creating behavioral routines that last.

The second major shortcoming of willpower is that it's only useful in the short run. Remember, creating and sustaining a new routine, whether it involves flossing your teeth, reading non-fiction, or doing pushups, requires consistent application.

You have to execute on a regular basis to make the routine stick.

The problem is, as noted earlier, willpower burns brightly in the beginning, but fades quickly. This means you can't rely on it. Your personal store of willpower will often be empty, leaving you vulnerable to temptations that derail your efforts to develop new habits.

This is one of the most common reasons so many people find it difficult to develop new, lasting behavioral patterns. New behaviors are easy to create, but nearly impossible to sustain through willpower alone. Unfortunately, too many people rely on it without realizing its inherently limited, easily-depleted, short-term nature. Consequently, they unwittingly sabotage their efforts from the outset.

In the next section, titled *Why Habits Will Always Trump Willpower*, I'll describe the simplest, most effective way to make new routines stick.

Why Habits Will
Always Trump Willpower

If neither motivation nor willpower will help you to create and sustain new behavioral patterns, what's the solution?

It's simple: small habits.

As we noted in *Part II: Triggers, Routines, Rewards, And Loops*, triggers prompt behaviors that result in rewards. These are loops.

But the behaviors, or routines, in these loops are not yet habits. Turning them into habits requires consistent application.

As we discussed, motivation is temporary and fleeting. It comes and goes, and therefore you can't rely on it.

Willpower is an expression of self-control. In resolving to do one thing (mow the lawn, go for a jog, etc.), we must resist the temptation to do more appealing things (watch television, take a nap, etc.). But recall that willpower is a finite resource that is steadily depleted from the moment we wake up in the morning. Thus, like motivation, you can't count on it.

But consider what happens when you create a habit. It becomes an integral part of your daily experience, often to the point that you do it without thinking about it. You don't weigh it against other options. Nor do you go through an internal debate regarding whether you have enough energy to perform the habit. It's a part of your life, and you execute accordingly.

For example, you brush your teeth each morning. You don't think about doing it. You simply do it. It's an ingrained habit and part of your daily experience. You don't have to be motivated to brush your teeth. Nor do you need to exert willpower to do it. It simply gets done.

This is true for any habit you've developed, from putting on your seatbelt when you climb into a vehicle to typing without looking at your keypad. You do these things without thinking about them. They're entrenched in your mind.

This is the reason habits, even tiny ones, will always trump willpower and motivation with respect to making new routines last. They become so deeply rooted over time that you feel uncomfortable when you neglect to perform them.

For example, try to recall the last time you left your home in the morning after forgetting to brush your teeth. You probably felt unsettled, even if you weren't immediately aware of the reason.

That's the power of habits. Once you form them, they're unshakeable.

In *Part IV: 10 Steps To Forming Healthy Habits That Last!*, I'll give you a simple, step-by-step plan for developing any habit you can imagine.

This is where the rubber meets the road.

Part IV

10 Steps To Forming Healthy Habits That Last!

This is the material you've been waiting for. The details leading up to this point set the stage for the habit development plan I'm about to give you. Your familiarity with triggers, routines, rewards, motivation, and willpower will prove critical to your success in adopting and sustaining new habits.

I've organized this 10-step plan so that each step is easy to apply. Each step is simple, but essential to making the plan work. Skip one and you risk sabotaging your efforts.

Read through Part IV in its entirety. Then, revisit steps as needed, either for inspiration or reminders regarding why they're important.

Here's how you'll benefit: this simple 10-step plan will help you to develop any positive habit you desire.

Do you want to start exercising? This is how you do it.

Do you want to start reading non-fiction books? This plan will show you how.

Would you like to start eating better and drinking more water? You're about to learn a fail-proof strategy.

Are you interested in increasing your productivity, being

more organized, saving more money, or becoming more social? This 10-step plan is the answer.

As you'll see in the following pages, it's a surefire strategy for forming new behaviors that last.

Step 1: Clarify The Goal You Want To Achieve With Your New Habit

Before you rush into developing a new habit, it's important to know *why* you want to do so. As I mentioned in *Part I: How Developing Healthy Habits Improves Your Quality Of Life*, we act with purpose. We do things for specific reasons, even if we don't think about those reasons.

For example, we brush our teeth each day out of habit. We do so to keep them clean, prevent the onset of cavities, and freshen our breath. These outcomes constitute our purpose.

It's the same with any activity we pursue, from exercising and dieting to organizing our desks and cleaning the kitchen. We act with purpose. We act with intent.

With that in mind, first identify the specific outcome you'd like to enjoy. What do you want to achieve?

For example, suppose you want to lose 20 pounds. The weight loss is merely a means to an end (or possibly multiple ends). Specifically, you want to enjoy more energy during the day, look slimmer, feel better, and protect yourself against heart disease. These are your desired outcomes. They inform the types of habits you'll pursue.

Many people try to develop new behavioral patterns without giving much consideration to the *specific* goals they hope to achieve with them. They often have little more than a vague idea. For example, they may want to "get into shape" or "be healthier." But their goals lack specificity. Consequently, they rush into habits that are poorly suited for them.

You can do better.

Before you choose habits to adopt, figure out what you'd like to achieve as a result of adopting them. Be specific. For example, don't merely say you'd like to lose weight. Determine the number of pounds you'd like to lose as well as the reasons you'd like to lose them.

Once you know your desired outcome, proceed to Step 2 with confidence that you'll choose the habits that best complement it.

Step 2: Identify The Habit You Want To Develop

Now that you've clarified your goal, you can boldly pick habits that'll streamline the process of achieving it. You won't run the risk of choosing new behaviors that slow the process down or worse, derail your efforts entirely.

For example, suppose you'd like to lose weight. As noted in the previous section, this is a vague goal that begs clarification. *Why* do you want to lose the weight? What do you hope to achieve in doing so?

Let's further suppose that you decide to skip Step 1. Instead, you immediately pick a habit you believe will help you to shed the extra pounds.

The problem here is that you might pick a habit that helps you to lose weight, but sabotages your long-term objective - for example, to feel better or have more energy. There are many weight loss strategies that can damage your long-term health and negatively impact the way you feel in the process.

The good news is that if you've completed Step 1, you've already clarified your objective. You know exactly what you'd like to achieve. Picking a new habit - importantly, the *right* habit - to effect that goal becomes a piece of cake.

Using our weight loss example, let's say your goal is to enjoy more energy in the afternoon, the time of day when mental fatigue typically sets in. Following are a few small habits that will help:

- Go to bed 30 minutes earlier each night.
- Eat a light lunch.
- Avoid sugary snacks. Choose snacks with protein.
- Do five pushups during each afternoon break.
- Stay hydrated.
- Reduce your afternoon work sessions to 30 minutes. Take 5-minute breaks between them. Stretch your muscles or take a walk.

Notice how some of these habits aren't directly related to losing weight. Instead, they address your main objective, the *reason* you want to lose weight. They help you to sustain your energy levels and avoid the afternoon slump. As a bonus, they'll also help you to drop the extra pounds.

This example demonstrates the importance of clarifying your goal before choosing a new habit. Doing so allows you to pick the *right* habit for the job.

In Step 3, we'll talk about how to make sure you perform your new routine on a regular basis.

Step 3: Break Down Your New Habit To Its Smallest Iteration

The biggest obstacle to performing any new habit is that we often make it too daunting. It takes so much effort to perform it that we feel discouraged.

For example, I've tried many times in the past to incorporate pushups as a form of daily exercise. I failed over and over. My problem was that I had in mind a "reasonable" number of pushups that would help me to get into shape. The number was 50.

I hadn't done pushups for years. Doing 10 in a row required a suspension of disbelief, much less 50. In my defense, I tried. It wasn't pretty. My arms wobbled uncontrollably after the seventh pushup.

Ultimately, I gave up. Not once. Not twice. Several times. I figured that if I couldn't even do 10 pushups, what was the point?

That perspective was entirely wrongheaded. My problem wasn't that I was unable to do more than a few pushups. My problem was that I wasn't giving myself permission to start small.

Starting small removes resistance. It obliterates discouragement and spurs us to take action. In *Part I: How Developing Healthy Habits Improves Your Quality Of Life*, I mentioned that I now do 25 pushups a day. I *didn't* mention that they're relatively easy for me at this point. Here's the key: I didn't start with 25. I gave myself permission to start small, doing just five pushups a day. I increased the number by increments of one each week.

That removed any excuse I might have had to start. I could do five pushups, even if the sight of my doing them made observers cringe. And importantly, I required neither willpower nor motivation. I just needed to start small.

Leo Babauta, who runs the popular website ZenHabits.net, once said the following about adopting new habits:

"Make it so easy you can't say no."

In other words, break your new habit down to its smallest iteration. If you're trying to do pushups, start with five (or even one). If you're trying to drink more water, start with a few extra ounces. If you're trying to get up earlier in the morning, set your alarm five minutes ahead of the time you normally wake up.

Give yourself permission to start small. You'll find that doing so will erase any internal resistance you feel about starting at all.

Next up: selecting a reliable cue that prompts you to perform your new habit.

Step 4: Create A Cue
To Trigger The Habit

As I mentioned in the section *How Triggers And Routines Lead To New Habits* (see Part II), triggers (or cues) precede all learned behaviors - at least in the beginning. The most important thing to remember is that we control them. We set the circumstances that spur us to take action.

For example, if you want to start jogging each morning, you might position your running shoes next to your bed. Seeing them upon waking would be the trigger that prompts you to jog. If you want to keep your workstation clean, you might clear it off right before you leave your office each day. In this case, 5:00 p.m. (or whenever you leave the office) is your trigger.

I mentioned that I use Chopin's Prelude in E Minor Op. 28, No. 4 as a trigger to start writing. I'm listening to it as I'm writing this section. I arrived at my local coffeeshop 20 minutes ago, cued the track on my Macbook, and immediately got to work.

Identify an activity or sequence of activities that can serve as a trigger for *your* new habit. Research suggests the best approach is to choose an *existing* routine to serve as the cue for a new one.

In 2011, the journal Psychology, Health & Medicine published a study examining different approaches to forming new habits and making them stick. The authors found that linking the new habits to existing ones proved to be the most effective path. They noted *"the new behaviors were often embedded in existing routines and their predictability, stability and order was particularly conducive to integration of new behaviors."*

Think about the new habit you want to form. What do you currently do by ritual that can serve as its trigger?

For example, suppose you'd like to start taking short walks each day (a good, low-impact form of exercise). You might use meals as triggers; each time you finish a meal, go for a 10-minute walk. Or you could use time as a trigger (though experts are divided regarding its effectiveness). You might schedule walks at 10:00 a.m., 12:30 p.m., 4:00 p.m., and 7:00 p.m.

If you want to start flossing your teeth on a daily basis, use the act of *brushing* your teeth as a trigger. Floss immediately after you brush. The former will eventually become an automatic response to the latter.

The cues you choose will help you to overcome the inevitable internal resistance you'll experience as you form new habits. When you're tired, unmotivated, and lack the willpower to do more than sit on your couch and watch television, they'll spur you to take action.

If you don't have an existing routine you can use to cue your new habit, create one. While doing so is less effective than using an existing routine, it's the next best option.

Use time, location, or even your emotional state.

For example, suppose you want to get into the habit of saying hello to strangers. You may not have an existing routine that can trigger this behavior. But you can *create* one based on location. Here's how:

Commit to greeting at least one stranger each time you visit your local grocery store. Or promise yourself that you'll say hello to one stranger while standing in line at Starbucks. Over time, this location-based routine will automatically cue your new habit.

In the next section, we'll discuss how to create a progressive plan for your new habit.

Step 5: Establish A Clear Objective

This step is simple. But it's one of the most important steps of the habit formation process. In fact, Step 6 is completely dependent on it.

Here, you assign a numeric value to your new habit. This value will help you to come up with a plan for building the habit, and allow you to monitor your progress along the way.

Let me explain…

Suppose you want to start doing pushups. As we noted in Step 3, you should start small. Don't start with a goal of 50 per day if you're a couch potato (I speak from experience). Instead, start with five. You can do five. Your arms might shake a bit, but you won't die.

Five is your numeric value for this new habit. It gives you a set-in-stone starting point. It defines whether or not you have successfully performed the new habit on any given day. If you do three pushups, you know that you'll have to perform two more before you can claim success.

This sounds simple, and perhaps even pedestrian. But it's a critical step toward forming behavioral patterns that persist in the face of obstacles. You need a number that defines daily success.

Here are a few more examples to drive this point home:

New habit: say hello to strangers.

Numeric value: say hello to *three* strangers each day.

New habit: meditate.

Numeric value: meditate for *60* seconds each morning.

New habit: write a personal journal.

Numeric value: write for *five* minutes each evening.

You get the idea. The numbers define success in an irrefutable manner. There's no ambiguity. They specify when the habit has been successfully performed for the day.

Up next: we're going to build a plan for *expanding* your new habit.

Step 6: Design A Plan To Slowly Increase Your New Habit

Some habits are daily, one-time affairs. You're not interested in increasing the number of repetitions. You just want to make sure that you do it each day.

An example is flossing your teeth. You want to make sure it gets done each morning or evening (or both). You're not interested in doing it *20 times* a day.

Other habits are perfectly suited for increasing the number of repetitions or the amount of time allotted to them each day. Here are some examples:

- Pushups
- Drinking water
- Taking walks
- Reading non-fiction
- Pitching potential clients
- Following up with leads
- Writing a journal
- Meditating
- Greeting strangers

Don't assume you'll naturally increase your habit over time. Create a plan for doing so. Otherwise, internal resistance and external obstacles will almost certainly get in your way.

Let's use our pushups example from the previous section for illustration. You'll recall that we started with five pushups per day. That number, our daily objective, is so small that it's difficult to say no.

Let's suppose you want to do 50 pushups per day. Here's a hypothetical plan that will help you to work up to that point:

Week 1: do 5 pushups

Week 2: do 8 pushups

Week 3: do 11 pushups

Week 4: do 14 pushups

Week 5: do 17 pushups

Week 6: do 20 pushups

Week 7: do 23 pushups

Week 8: do 26 pushups

Week 9: do 29 pushups

Week 10: do 32 pushups

Week 11: do 35 pushups

Week 12: do 38 pushups

Week 13: do 41 pushups

Week 14: do 44 pushups

Week 15: do 47 pushups

Week 16: do 50 pushups

Sixteen weeks. Four months. This may seem like a lot of time to reach your goal (50 pushups per day), but the weeks will pass quickly. At the end of the fourth month, you'll look back and be astonished at your progress.

The important point is that you create a firm plan to reach your goal. Without a plan, you'll be forced to rely on your motivation, willpower, and mood to increase your new habit.

That's setting yourself up for failure.

You'll notice that the incremental increases in our hypothetical plan are small. We're increasing the number of pushups by only three each week. This approach is consistent with the core theme of *Small Habits Revolution*. Starting small and making incremental progress wins the day.

In the next section, we'll create a reward system that'll inspire you to sustain your habit over the long run.

Step 7: Create A Simple Reward System

You'll recall from the section *How Rewards Reinforce Newly-Formed Habits* that positive reinforcement plays an important role in habit development. As I noted, everything we do is motivated by some type of reward, either received immediately (e.g. praise) or in the future (e.g. a promotion).

Rewards are a powerful tool when developing new behaviors. The more positive they are, the more they inspire us to act. Thus, it's worth creating a reward system to aid you in developing whatever new habit you choose to pursue.

How do you choose a reward that'll serve as inspiration and won't sabotage your efforts?

First, make it small.

Suppose you're developing the habit of cleaning your desk at the end of each workday. Don't reward yourself with an expensive dinner at your favorite steakhouse. Instead, treat yourself to your favorite candy bar (opt for the smaller "fun size" if you're watching your weight).

Research shows that small rewards are just as effective as large ones when it comes to developing new behaviors. In fact, they're *more* effective since you can enjoy them immediately. Gratification without delay is a crucial aspect of positive reinforcement.

Second, make sure your reward doesn't work against you.

Suppose you're trying to jog each day, in part to lose weight. It would make little sense to reward yourself with a donut after each jog. The donut would undermine your goal.

Third, experiment. Not every reward will be equally motivating to you. Some will be more compelling than others. For example, you may find that calling a friend is a bigger motivator than eating a candy bar. If so, make the phone call your reward for performing your chosen habit. Likewise, you might find that taking a short walk is more enjoyable to you than taking a catnap. If so, go for a walk immediately after performing your new routine.

It's only by experimenting with different rewards that you'll find the one that works best for you.

Over time, you'll see patterns in the types of rewards that inspire you. For example, you might notice that you're motivated by fun activities (short walks, swimming, etc.) more than food. You may notice that spending time with friends (on the phone, meeting for coffee, etc.) is a bigger incentive than solo activities. As you develop new habits throughout your life, picking rewards that truly inspire you will become second nature.

Don't underestimate the power of a good incentive. It can play an integral role in forming any new behavioral pattern.

In Step 8, I'll share a simple hack that'll help you to sustain any new habit you pursue.

Step 8: Perform The Habit At The Same Time Each Day

Think about the things you do at the same time each day. Here are a few examples:

- Brush your teeth
- Take a shower
- Eat lunch
- Go to the gym
- Watch your favorite television show
- Take a smoke break
- Make coffee
- Go for a jog

These activities are ingrained in your mind. You do them without thinking about them. They're a part of your daily process. As such, failing to do one of them can put you in a state of unease.

That's an important feature of these daily habits. You do them at the same time each day. That, in turn, causes them into evolve into automatic responses to established triggers.

For example, suppose you take a smoke break at 10:00 a.m. each morning. You've been doing so for years. As such, when the clock strikes 10:00 a.m., you instinctively get up and go outside with a cigarette behind your ear. It's automatic. Time -

in this case, 10:00 a.m. - is the trigger.

Or suppose the first thing you do when you wake up in the morning is stumble over to your coffeemaker and turn it on. Here, the trigger is the act of waking up and getting out of bed. The response, turning on your coffeemaker, is automatic. It's a deep-rooted habit.

Leverage this tactic with any new behavior you want to develop. For example, if you intend to do 10 pushups each day, do them at 7:00 a.m., before you leave for your office. If you plan to read non-fiction for 15 minutes each day, do it during your lunch break. If you aim to declutter your desk each day, do it at the end of the workday.

In other words, perform the new routine at the same time each day. Do it like clockwork. Put it on your daily calendar and assign a time for the activity, even if it only requires a few moments.

You'll be tempted to adjust the time every now and then to suit your circumstances or emotional state (e.g. *"I don't feel like doing pushups right now. I'll do them later."*). Resist the temptation. Performing your routine at the same time each day causes it to become an automatic response to its associated trigger. You'll eventually perform it without thinking about it. That's when your routine becomes an entrenched habit that sticks.

Next up: we'll discuss some of the roadblocks you'll face in developing and sustaining new habits.

Step 9: Identify The Stumbling Blocks That Can Sabotage You

The main theme of *Small Habits Revolution* is to start with habits that are so small that it's difficult to say no. Instead of doing 25 pushups at the outset, start with five (or just one). Instead of jogging a mile, start with 50 yards. Instead of reading several chapters of a non-fiction book, start with three pages.

You get the idea.

Unfortunately, no matter how small the habit, internal and external forces will conspire against you.

Your mind will try to persuade you to neglect your new routine in favor of more enjoyable activities - for example, taking a nap or watching TV.

Unanticipated circumstances may make it inconvenient to perform your habit. For example, a broken shoestring may undermine your intent to go jogging. A dead laptop battery may prevent you from writing your daily journal entry.

Whenever you form a new habit, it's important to recognize the obstacles that stand between you and success. Anticipate them. Prepare for them.

For example, suppose you want to get into the habit of jogging each day. Your mind will occasionally try to convince you that skipping a day will make you feel better. It will try to persuade you to watch television, enjoy a bowl of ice cream, or log onto Facebook instead. If you recognize in advance that this will happen, you'll be better prepared to resist the temptations.

In the same way, realize that circumstances outside your control may also conspire against you. I mentioned a broken shoestring above as an example. Your plan to go jogging might also be waylaid by rain, a power outage, or an urgent phone call from your boss. If you acknowledge in advance that such things can happen, you'll be less inclined to abandon your habit in frustration.

Starting small and building slowly is a proven strategy for developing new behavioral patterns. But you'll still face stumbling blocks that threaten to derail your efforts. Identify them ahead of time. You'll be ready to deal with them in a productive fashion that doesn't impair your long-term success.

In the final step, we'll talk about one of the most important facets of any habit development plan: monitoring your progress.

Step 10: Monitor Your Progress Once A Week

This is a simple step, but one that's often overlooked or dismissed entirely. A lot of people try to adopt new habits without a system for keeping track of their progress.

It's understandable. Tracking their progress requires time and effort. With so much going on in our lives, there's little incentive to do it. But tracking your progress is the only way to measure how you're doing according to your initial plans.

Recall my own example of trying to reach 50 pushups a day. I started with five a day, increasing the number by one each week. I'm now at 25 a day. The progress I've made - it's progress for *me*, anyway - is largely due to my tracking system. It has kept me accountable.

My system isn't complicated. In fact, it's surprisingly simple. I maintain a spreadsheet with two columns. The first column is the date. The second column is the number of pushups completed for the corresponding date. I can see at a glance how far I've come and how far I have yet to go to achieve my end goal (50 pushups a day).

Monitoring your progress does four things for you. First, it provides motivation. The more headway you make, the more inspired you'll feel to continue performing your new routine.

Second, it shows the regularity of your habit. You'll be reminded that it should be performed daily, which reinforces it as a behavioral pattern.

Third, tracking your progress demonstrates what you can achieve. When I first started doing pushups, the idea of doing 25 pushups in a row was laughable. Today, it's easy. I know with steady progress - one additional pushup each week - I'll eventually be able to do 50 pushups without breaking a sweat.

Fourth, when it comes to adopting new habits, good intentions are not enough. Action is required. A tracking system will push you to take action on a daily basis.

There are numerous apps that will help you to track your progress when developing new routines. Personally, I prefer spreadsheets. First, they're simple and do the job perfectly well. Second, I don't have to clutter my phone with more apps. Third, they're free (I use Google Sheets).

If you must use an app to track your habits, here are several I've seen others recommend:

- 42Goals.com
- Chains.cc
- HabitGrams.com
- LifeTick.com
- 21Habit.com
- StridesApp.com
- HabitList.com
- Coach.me

Full disclosure: I've never used any of the above apps. I mention them only because other people seem to like them and you might have a similarly positive experience.

The main point is that you keep an eye on your progress

whenever you develop a new habit. It doesn't matter whether you use spreadsheets, an app, or a pen and legal pad. As long as you're tracking things.

You now have a simple, proven 10-step system for adopting any new habit you can imagine. It works. But as they say, the proof is in the pudding. I'm willing to bet that if you apply the system as I've described, you'll note its effectiveness from the outset.

It's normal to experience internal resistance whenever you pursue a new habit. Our brains like routine and dislike change. In Part V, we'll talk about tactics you can use to streamline the process.

Part V

Seven Rules For Setting Yourself Up For Success

Adopting new, healthy habits is difficult work. You know this from experience. If you've ever tried to maintain a healthy diet, exercise on a daily basis, or keep a daily journal, you know how hard it can be to make the practice stick.

In the previous section, I mentioned the role of internal resistance. The brain naturally resists change. It prefers to maintain the status quo, which makes starting and sustaining new habits difficult.

The seven rules we're going to cover in this section will help you to overcome this natural resistance. They'll make the habit development process easier and streamline adopting new behavioral patterns that last.

Rule #1: Start Small

In 2005, Fast Company published an article examining our unwillingness to change, even in the face of potentially devastating circumstances. One expert noted that among patients who underwent coronary bypass surgery, fewer than 10% modified their lifestyles to accommodate their flagging health (https://www.fastcompany.com/52717/change-or-die).

This behavior is universal. Internal resistance stems from how the brain works. The bigger the change in behavior, the more resistance you'll experience.

This is the reason you should start small when pursuing a new habit. Doing so reduces internal resistance. You're not asking your brain to accept a radical change; you're asking it to accept a tiny one that will grow over time. It requires a smaller investment.

As Leo Babauta says, "*make it so easy [your brain] can't say no.*"

I've presented examples of starting small throughout this book. Here are a few more ideas to drive the point home:

New Habit: Flossing your teeth.

Start small: Floss one tooth. Floss an additional tooth every three days.

New Habit: Eat more vegetables.

Start small: Eat a small veggie (for example, one-fourth of a carrot). Increase the portion size, or add another small veggie, every three or four days.

New Habit: Jog five miles a day.

Start small: Jog 50 yards. Add 50 yards each week.

New Habit: Practice playing the guitar each day.

Start small: Practice for five minutes a day. Add five minutes to each practice session with each passing week.

New Habit: Keep in touch with friends.

Start small: Send one email to a friend each week. Increase the number to two per week after the first month.

The point is to take baby steps. These small steps will turn into big strides down the road. The important thing is that they'll help you get started when your brain's natural response to any type of behavioral change is to put up resistance.

The smaller you start, the less you'll struggle in adopting and sustaining your new routine.

Rule #2: Commit To Performing Your New Habit For 30 Days

It's easy to stick to a new habit for two or three days. Anyone can do five pushups on Monday, five on Tuesday, and five on Wednesday. The real test is whether the routine sticks over the long run.

That takes commitment.

Personally, I love the idea of a 30-day challenge. Thirty days is a nice, round number that complements the use of a calendar. Studies also show that with daily application, it's long enough to reinforce any new behavioral pattern.

You've probably heard that it takes 21 days to form a new habit. That claim stems from remarks made by author and cosmetic surgeon Dr. Maxwell Maltz. Dr. Maltz noted that patients who underwent cosmetic surgery would require 21 days to become accustomed to their new appearance.

Notice that the good doctor wasn't referring to the adoption of new habits. Despite this fact, his remarks have been strangely co-opted to describe the process of habit development.

The truth is, there's no definite duration over which a new routine takes hold. Much depends on the type of routine, the level of internal resistance experienced, and the process by which the habit is adopted.

Thirty days is a reasonable number to focus on. It doesn't guarantee you'll stick to a new routine once you perform it for

30 days in a row. But it demonstrates that you're *capable* of doing so.

Once you've performed a habit for 30 days in a row, particularly if you do so at the same time each day following the same trigger, it's relatively easy to continue. It will have become a part of your daily process. It will have become deeply rooted in your mind as an activity you simply *do*, rather than having to *think* about doing.

In addition, a 30-day challenge gives you a tangible goal to shoot for. Why not make it fun? Turn it into a game whereby you receive a desired reward for successfully completing the 30-day cycle.

Thirty days is a useful marker. It'll signal that you've turned your new routine into a veritable habit, one that can last a lifetime.

Rule #3: Develop One Habit At A Time

One of the reasons so many people give up on their New Year's resolutions is because they try to do too much at once. For example, they want to:

- Eat better
- Start exercising
- Lose weight
- Learn new skills
- Get organized
- Find a mate
- Buy a house
- Start doing yoga
- Read more non-fiction books
- Dress with more style
- Save money
- Learn a new language

You get the idea. It's no wonder so many people abandon their resolutions early in the new year. There are simply too many behavioral changes to pursue. Failure is practically guaranteed.

For this reason, I strongly recommend you adopt one new habit at a time. Two at the most. Resist the temptation to tackle several at once. Developing good habits isn't a sprint; it's a marathon. You have the rest of your life to adopt them. Don't rush through multiple positive routines, and sabotage your long-term success in the process.

If you try to develop multiple habits at the same time, you'll end up feeling overwhelmed. Each one will feel like a chore, even if you start small. They'll feel like a burden, which is the precise feeling this strategy is designed to prevent.

When you limit yourself to pursuing a single habit, you're able to focus on it. All of your energy is devoted to planting this single routine and allowing its roots to grow deep. The deeper the roots, the more likely you'll be performing the routine months, even years, down the road.

When can you confidently pursue a second habit? I suggest 30 days. As I noted in the previous section, a habit performed for 30 days in a row becomes firmly established. At that point, you can introduce another behavioral change without affecting the consistency with which you perform the first one.

Pursuing new habits in this manner may seem like slow progress. And in truth, it is. But imagine, in one year, you'll have made 12 healthy habits a deeply-rooted part of your life. If you adopt two habits per month, you'll have developed 24 positive habits.

That's a life-changing improvement by any measure! It's definitely more progress than 99% of people make toward adopting new behaviors in any given year.

There's an important bonus related to this strategy: your new habits will stick over the long run because you took the time to develop them slowly. They grow deep roots, becoming ingrained and eliminating internal resistance.

Consider the practice of brushing your teeth. You experience zero resistance to it. Formed over several years, the habit has developed unshakable, unbreakable roots.

So it will be with any new habit developed over time with singular focus.

Rule #4: Disclose Your New Habit To Others

Public accountability can be a powerful incentive to succeed. No one wants to fail in front of other people, especially friends and loved ones.

When you tell others about a new habit you intend to adopt, you become accountable to them. They'll ask you about your progress on occasion. They'll check in to see whether you've met your goal.

Your friends and family members don't mean to badger you. On the contrary, most of them will be interested in your progress because you're important to them. They'll root for your success.

Many people are uncomfortable involving their friends and family members. Perhaps their loved ones are cynical and more inclined to discourage them than cheer their success. Maybe their friends are likely to mock them when they fall of the wagon rather than encourage them to get up, dust themselves off, and move forward.

If you relate to this problem, don't despair. You can still benefit from public accountability in ways that don't involve those who are closest to you.

For example, reveal your habit-related goal on Facebook. Post weekly updates with your progress. Assuming you've chosen your friends well, they'll encourage you with each update. (Unfriend those who mock your efforts.)

Another option is to "hire" an accountability partner. This individual might be a family member who's consistently encouraging when you share a personal goal with him or her. It could be your closest friend who wants you to succeed in everything you do. It can be an acquaintance at your workplace.

If possible, pick someone who wants to improve himself or herself in some measurable way. You can serve as accountability partners for each other.

This person will provide motivational support as you develop and maintain your new routine. He or she will celebrate your triumphs. In the event you stumble, your partner will be there to encourage you to get back in the proverbial saddle.

He or she can also help you to identify reasons for failure, and brainstorm solutions. For example, suppose you want to get into the habit of jogging each evening. Your accountability partner may notice that you often complain that you lack energy. He or she might suggest jogging in the morning, when your energy level is higher.

Adopting any new behavior is difficult, especially when you do it alone. Being accountable to others, even just a single person, can mean the difference between success and failure.

Tell someone about your plans. Make that individual aware regarding what you intend to achieve. If you're like me, you'll find that doing so inspires you to make sure you perform your new habit each day.

Rule #5: Perform Your New Habit Early In The Morning

I'm a morning person. I usually get up around 5:30 a.m. I used to be a night owl, but found that I have more energy and clarity (thanks coffee!) in the morning. I'm far more productive in the early hours, which allows me to relax during the afternoon and evening.

One thing I've noticed about myself is that I experience far less internal resistance in the morning. For example, when I want to write, my brain is less likely to put up a fight. I find it much easier to sit down, find my focus, and start writing at 6:00 a.m. than noon or 6:00 p.m.

I'd be willing to bet you're the same. You'll experience less internal resistance to your new routine if you do it in the morning than if you wait until the afternoon or evening.

Have you ever arrived home from work, tired and beat, and had to fight an internal battle to get yourself to the gym? Did some of those battles end with you plopping yourself on your couch and turning on the television? If so, you have firsthand experience with what I'm referring to.

It's for this reason that I recommend performing your new habit in the morning. You'll have more energy and deal with less internal friction.

The earlier, the better. Mornings can quickly spiral out of control. That's partly due to the fact that we tend to overestimate the amount of free time we have available.

Perform your new habit as early as is reasonable. If you're trying to develop the habit of jogging, do it right after you wake up. Likewise with journaling, reading non-fiction, practicing yoga, and any other habit you choose to incorporate into your life.

Again, be reasonable. If you want to get into the habit of calling your parents three times a week, do it later in the morning. It won't do you any good to call them more often if they're always irritated because you keep waking them up!

Mornings are an ideal time to perform most new behaviors. If you're an early riser, you'll be able to focus on them while everyone else is still asleep.

Rule #6: Remind Yourself
Of Your Reasons

In *Part I: How Developing Healthy Habits Improves Your Quality Of Life,* I noted that everything we do begins with a purpose. We exercise to look and feel better. We diet to lose weight. We read non-fiction to expand our horizons and increase our knowledge.

But it's easy to forget our reasons for adopting new habits even as we perform them each and every day. With time and repetition, we begin to focus more on the trees (e.g. new routines) while losing sight of the forest (e.g. our initial purpose).

This tendency can impair our ability to sustain new habits. Our purpose drives us to take action. When we lose sight of it, we become less inclined to act.

For this reason, set aside time once a week to remind yourself of the reasons that inspired you to adopt your new habit in the first place.

For example, you might be learning a new language in order to communicate more easily with your in-laws. You may be trying to get into the habit of decluttering your workspace so you can be more productive and enjoy more free time in the evenings. You might be building the habit of striking up conversations with strangers to improve your interpersonal skills.

Every habit you pursue is preceded by a reason. Whether this reason is to become healthier, more confident, more social, more supportive, or more knowledgable, it's what inspired you to adopt the habit in the first place.

Don't assume you'll remember the reason. The brain has a tendency to put such things on a cognitive shelf as it devotes attention to more immediate concerns (such as performing your new habit).

Be proactive. Pick one day a week and spend a few minutes to remind yourself about the reasons you want to pursue your desired behaviors. Ask yourself *why* you want to change.

It's worth noting that your reasons for adopting a particular routine may change as time passes. For example, suppose you start exercising because your doctor warned you about the dangers of a sedentary lifestyle. But over time, as you continue jogging, doing pushups, and lifting weights, you discover that exercise gives you more energy and helps you to sleep better. Your reasons to continue the routine shift as you experience previously unidentified benefits.

Conducting a weekly review brings these new reasons to light. In doing so, it refocuses your attention on factors that are important to you. It's a good investment of your time.

Rule #7: Be Willing To Forgive Yourself If You Fail

Occasional failures are almost guaranteed. Anticipate them. When they happen, forgive yourself and get back in the saddle.

Failure can happen for a variety of reasons. When you start with tiny habits, the most common reason is forgetfulness.

When I first started doing pushups, the activity sometimes slipped my mind. You'll recall that I started by doing only five pushups per day. They took 20 seconds to perform. Because the task was so small, I made the mistake of not writing it down on my daily to-do list. Consequently, I forgot to do them on occasion.

Forgetfulness caused me to fail over and over.

Here's the most salient point: I didn't berate myself for my negligence. There was no value in doing so. Instead, I forgave myself and renewed my commitment. I then identified the reason for my failure, resolved it (I added the activity to Todoist so I would be reminded to do it each morning), and moved forward.

I strongly encourage you to do the same.

Don't beat yourself up when you stumble. Don't spend time blaming yourself. There's no value in doing so. Casting blame will only discourage you from continuing. And remember, this is a marathon rather than a sprint. The day-to-day is merely a stepping stone to effecting long-term behavioral change.

Realize that slip-ups and missteps are inevitable. Be ready to pardon yourself when they occur. Then, get up, dust yourself off, and get back on track.

Don't allow the setbacks of the past to sabotage your future success. Keep moving forward. Tomorrow brings a new opportunity to incorporate positive, lasting change in your life.

Part VI

How To Guarantee
Your New Habits Will Last

Let's do a quick recap.

You now have a simple 10-step system for adopting any new habit you wish to make a part of your life. You also know several tips and hacks that will streamline the habit development process.

In Part VI, we'll cover numerous ways to ensure your new behaviors stick. I've mentioned a couple of them in previous sections. I'll go into more detail about them here and introduce several new ideas that will help turn your desired routines into lifelong habits.

Why New Habits Often Fail To Stick

Before we discuss strategies that'll help guarantee your new habits stick, it's important to understand why most people have trouble in this area. There are seven reasons.

First, the desired routine or behavior represents too big a change. As I noted earlier, big changes produce internal resistance. The main theme of *Small Habits Revolution* is to start with a routine that's so small that internal resistance is all but nonexistent.

Second, many people beat themselves up when they fail to maintain their new habits. Their self-flagellation only discourages them from moving forward.

A third reason new habits fail to last is because the individual sets his or her sights on the outcome rather than the routine itself. Our brains respond to consistent application. This is the reason routines performed each day at the same time of day, prompted by the same triggers, become deeply-rooted habits. By contrast, when our focus shifts from the routine to the outcome, we lose momentum and our responses to specific triggers become less automatic.

Fourth, we lose track of our reasons for adopting new routines. Without clearly-defined reasons for continuing, we lose sight of our purpose and eventually abandon our new, positive behaviors.

Fifth, many people fail to maintain good habits because they neglect to create a supportive environment. For example, the individual who wants to start jogging in the morning continues to wake up late. The person who wishes to stick to a healthy diet keeps cookies, chips, and ice cream in the house. Environment plays an important role in determining whether a habit takes hold.

A sixth reason habits fail to stick is because people often try to adopt too many at once. We discussed the importance of pursuing one habit at a time in *Part V: Seven Rules For Setting Yourself Up For Success* (Rule #3). Pursuing several at once is a recipe for failure.

Seventh, many people don't take their habits seriously. They start with good intentions, but are not fully committed to them. Failing to perform their new routines several days in a row is not a serious matter to them. As such, they're neither inclined to figure out the reason for their neglect nor motivated to seek a resolution. Their abandonment of their new routines is inevitable once they experience internal resistance.

You now know the problems to look for in the event you struggle to maintain your new habits. If you *do* struggle, review the seven reasons above. Check whether any of them describe your circumstances. If they do, take the necessary steps to resolve them.

Leverage The Power Of Accountability

We discussed the idea of accountability in *Part V: Seven Rules For Setting Yourself Up For Success* (Rule #4). It's worth revisiting here in the context of how to choose a good accountability partner. A good partner will encourage you as you develop new behaviors, and push you to transform them into lifelong habits.

There are five key factors to think about when selecting this individual.

First, he or she must be willing to give you honest, well-meaning feedback. Remember, you'll likely stumble on occasion. It won't do you any good to be accountable to someone who's unwilling to offer constructive, supportive feedback to help you get back on track.

Second, find someone who will sincerely support your efforts. For example, if you want to get into the habit of reading non-fiction books, choose someone who finds great joy in doing the same. This person will be enthused about your new habit and be more invested in your success.

Third, pick a partner who's willing to connect several times a week, and preferably each day. This allows you to give a daily report on your habit - specifically, whether or not you performed it that day.

It's helpful to schedule a time to connect. For example, text each other at noon each day if you intend to perform your new habit in the morning. Connect after the workday ends if you intend to perform it during your lunch break.

Fourth, choose an accountability partner who will challenge you. For example, suppose you want to eventually do 25 pushups a day (starting with just five per day). Once you reach 25, a good partner will ask whether you've thought about progressing to 30. And then 35. And so on.

Fifth, if possible, select a partner who's trying to adopt the same habit as you. For example, if you want to start jogging, be accountable to someone who wishes to do the same. In turn, this individual can make himself or herself accountable to you.

Imagine how encouraging it'll be to work with a trusted partner in developing the same habit at the same pace. You can keep each other on track with a daily text:

You: "Jogged my 500 yards this morning. How about you?"

Partner: "Me too! Are we still doing 600 yards tomorrow?"

You: "Absolutely! :)"

Partner: "Awesome. Have a great evening!"

Accountability can be both fun and inspiring. The key is to pick a partner who'll be consistent, supportive, and encouraging as you strive to turn your new behaviors into deep-seated habits.

Use Seinfeld's Calendar Strategy

Top comedians like Seinfeld make the art of telling jokes look easy. They stand on the stage and deliver one after another, seeming to pull from an endless trove of material. In reality, they spend a significant amount of time coming up with new material to share with their audiences.

In his early days, back when he was on the club circuit, Seinfeld developed a simple habit to ensure he never ran out of jokes. He wrote one joke a day.

An important part of his method involved setting up a large wall calendar that displayed the entire year on a single page. Once he wrote the current day's joke, he'd cross the day off the calendar with a red pen.

After a week of writing jokes, the calendar showed a short series of big red Xs. The unbroken chain motivated Seinfeld to continue.

With each passing day, the series of red Xs grew longer. Soon, Seinfeld was inspired to write his daily joke, if only to avoid breaking the chain.

This strategy is simple, elegant, and practical. It can be used for any habit you wish to adopt. Want to learn a new language? Master one word a day and cross the day off your calendar. Would you like to write daily in a personal journal? Write one paragraph a day and mark it off on the calendar. Interested in jogging? Jog 250 yards a day and cross the day off.

The point is that you record each day's success on a calendar so you can see the unbroken chain. Continue to do so as you increase your habit, either in duration or repetition. You'll find that the calendar, once it's filled with line after line of red Xs, is a powerful incentive to keep extending the chain.

I use this method myself. Each day, after I do my daily pushups, I grab my red pen and cross the day off my calendar. The calendar is in plain sight, taped to a wall in my office. I can attest to the fact that the unbroken chain of Xs is a potent incentive to drop and give myself 25.

Try Seinfeld's calendar strategy for yourself. Use it to transform your next tiny routine into an ingrained, lifelong habit.

Link Your New Habit To A Reliable Cue

We talked about the importance of triggers, or cues, in *Part II: Triggers, Routines, Rewards, And Loops.* You learned about the different types of triggers (time, location, state of mind, people, and preceding events), along with the role they play in prompting us to take action.

In Step #4 of *Part IV: 10 Steps To Forming Healthy Habits That Last!*, we broached the idea of choosing triggers that complement our goals. To use the example in that section, you could place your running shoes next to your bed if you intend to go jogging first thing in the morning. Seeing your shoes when you wake up would be a suitable trigger. Or you might floss your teeth immediately after brushing them. Brushing your teeth would complement flossing them. In both cases, the cue sets the stage for the new routine.

Trigger selection as an aspect of habit development is so critical that it's worth revisiting. Choosing the right triggers can mean the difference between performing your habit as an automatic response and fighting internal resistance each day.

The ideal trigger is one that you control. For example, *you* dictate the position of your running shoes. *You* decide whether or not to brush your teeth. These circumstances are not influenced by external factors. You control them.

That makes them reliable. You can count on them to occur. Whether you perform your habit on any given day is independent of other people and events.

Some cues will have a greater effect on you than others. It's important to test different cues to identify the ones that work best for you.

For example, let's say you want to get into the habit of doing pushups each day. You might experiment with the following triggers:

- Washing your face
- Drinking a glass of water
- Listening to your favorite Bon Jovi song
- Arriving home after a short walk
- A specific time (e.g. 7:15 a.m.)
- The end of a daily conference call
- Turning the television on to watch the morning news

After testing several triggers, you'll find that one soundly beats the others in spurring you to take action. That's the one you should use.

The most important aspect is that you control whether or not the trigger occurs. For example, if you live in an area that receives a considerable amount of rain, avoid using "arriving home after a short walk" as a cue to do your daily pushups. You can't control the weather. Consequently, there will be times when you're unable to take a walk, making it an unreliable trigger.

Don't underestimate the importance of cue selection when you incorporate new routines into your day.

Insert Your New Routine
Into An Existing Habit Stack

In the section *The Five Different Types Of Triggers* (Part II), I mentioned a strategy called habit stacking. It's the practice of anchoring new routines to existing habits. It's a powerful method for making new routines stick.

Here's how it works:

There are a myriad of things you do during the course of your day that you take for granted. You do them without thinking about them. Some are connected to, or stacked on top of, each other.

For example, consider your morning routine. Upon waking up, you might stumble to your bathroom to wash your face, brush your teeth, use the toilet, and take a shower. This series of activities is a habit stack.

When you climb out of the shower, you might dry off, get dressed, and blow dry your hair. This is another habit stack.

When you emerge from the bathroom, you might pour yourself a cup of coffee, toast a slice of bread, scramble a few eggs, and check your email. This is yet another stack.

You probably perform numerous such habit stacks each day, even if you rarely think about them. Your brain has formed connections between the individual habits, prompting you to perform each one as an automatic response to the one preceding it.

One of the most effective ways to develop a new habit is to insert it into an existing stack. Your brain will quickly create a new connection between the new routine and the habits that bookend it.

Let's illustrate this idea with our "pushups" example. Suppose you insert the activity into the second habit stack described above...

1. Climb out of the shower
2. Dry off
3. Get dressed
4. Blow dry your hair

This existing stack would turn into the following stack...

1. Climb out of the shower
2. Dry off
3. *Perform five pushups*
4. Get dressed
5. Blow dry your hair

The original stack is already deeply rooted in your brain. Each habit contained within it happens automatically due to consistent execution over a long period of time. Your brain can quickly establish a connection between your new routine and these existing habits, making it easy to adopt the former.

Most people find habit stacking to be a highly effective strategy for introducing new habits and making them stick. I recommend that you identify the current stacks you perform during each day. Then, pick one and insert your new routine into it.

Put Your New Habit On Your Daily Calendar Or To-Do List

In *Part V: Seven Rules For Setting Yourself Up For Success* (Rule #7), I mentioned that I often forgot to do my pushups while trying to develop the habit. It was a major failure on my part.

The solution was simple. I put the activity into Todoist (an online app) and assigned it the highest priority setting. The latter action ensured that it appeared at the top of my daily to-do list so I wouldn't miss it.

I also made the task recur automatically on each day's list so that I didn't have to add it manually.

This was crucial to my success in developing the habit. The task always appeared front and center, and thus I no longer forgot to do my pushups. That made it easier for my brain to establish and reinforce the activity as a part of my morning routine (or stack, if you will).

I strongly recommend you do the same. Whenever you pursue a new habit, put it on your calendar or daily to-do list. I like Todoist because it's intuitive, simple, and free. Additionally, I can create dozens of to-do lists and organize them by context. And as noted, I can set specific tasks to repeat according to any schedule I desire (e.g. every day at 7:15 a.m., every Tuesday, the twelfth of each month, etc.).

There are a lot of apps available that'll do the same thing. Here are a few options:

- Remember The Milk (rememberthemilk.com)
- Toodledo (toodledo.com)
- Momentum (momentumdash.com
- Checkvist (checkvist.com)
- Cheddar (cheddarapp.com)
- Wunderlist (wunderlist.com)
- Finish (getfinish.com)
- TickTick (ticktick.com)

That's barely scratching the surface.

Some of these apps are free. Others charge a small one-time fee. A few impose a small monthly fee. None will break the bank.

If you prefer to put your new habit onto a daily calendar, you'll never want for options. I've been using Google Calendar for years. I love its simplicity. And the fact that it's free is a point in its favor.

If Google Calendar fails to excite you, here are a few alternatives:

- Cal (any.do/cal/)
- Cozi (cozy.com)
- Jorte (jorte.com)
- Fantastical 2 (flexibits.com/fantastical)
- Apple Calendar (apple.com/osx/apps/#calendar)
- Calendars 5 (iTunes store)
- CloudCal (Google Play store)
- Business Calendar 2 (Google Play store)
- SmartDay (leftcoastlogic.com/smartday/)

Until mid-2016, Sunrise was one of the most popular calendar apps. Not only was it free, but like Google Calendar, it worked on both iOS and Android. Unfortunately, Microsoft bought it and closed it down.

Thankfully, you still have a lot of options.

Here's the most salient point: avoid relying on your memory. Put your new habit onto a daily calendar or daily to-do list. You'll never have to worry about forgetting to do it. And with daily execution, your brain will have a much easier time making the habit stick.

Reflect On The Positive Effects Of Your New Habit

At the risk of beating a dead horse, we act with purpose. This is critical to understand in the context of habit development. Everything we do, every action we take, is prompted by a specific intent.

So it is with proactively adopting new behaviors. We exercise to get into shape. We eat healthy foods to lessen the risk of heart and vascular problems. We read non-fiction to learn about subject matter that is a mystery to us.

Naturally, you expect to benefit in some defined way for each new habit you adopt. Perhaps you hope to achieve greater focus and productivity. Maybe you want to experience more energy during the workday. Perhaps you'd like to strengthen the relationships you share with your spouse and kids.

The benefits you hope to receive encourage you to take action each day. They inspire you to maintain the routines you believe will deliver them.

Unfortunately, it's easy to lose sight of the ways in which your new, positive behaviors will affect your life. When that happens, you become more inclined to give up. You become more likely to abandon the habits that will bring about your desired outcome.

In Step #10 of *Part IV: 10 Steps To Forming Healthy Habits That Last!*, I recommended you review your progress once a week. Doing so will motivate you, reveal the regularity of your new routine, and demonstrate what you can achieve. This review session is an ideal time to reflect on how your new routines will improve the quality of your life.

For example, how would raising your afternoon energy levels affect your productivity? How would eating healthy foods affect how you feel throughout the day? How might reading non-fiction books give you new insight into subject matter that fascinates you?

Recognizing how your life will improve after adopting a new habit will remind you of why you're making the effort. Whether it's to be healthier, happier, more confident, or more connected to your loved ones, the reminder can serve as a powerful incentive to act.

And that can help to eliminate internal resistance as you incorporate new, healthy routines into your daily experience.

You now have everything you need to develop positive, life-enriching habits. You can start at any time, including right now. If you're uncertain regarding the type of habits to pursue, read on. In Part VII, I'll describe 23 example habits to get you started.

Part VII

Example Habits You Can Develop Using The Small Habits Strategy

I've given you a complete, proven system for adopting any habit you choose to pursue. Millions of people have used some form of the 10-step strategy I described in this book to adopt new, positive routines that improved the quality of their lives.

You can experience the same success. The challenge is knowing where to start.

There are countless habits you can develop that'll enrich your life. But that can be as paralyzing as it is empowering.

To help you get started, I'll list 23 habits that can lead to a more rewarding lifestyle. My purpose isn't to dictate which habits to pursue. On the contrary, it's to give you a starting point from which to brainstorm routines that are likely to have the greatest impact on your life.

Let's jump in…

23 Small Habits
That Can Change Your Life

For each of the following routines, I'll provide a few thoughts on how to start small. After all, that *is* the main theme of *Small Habits Revolution*. Remember, the key is to start so small that it's difficult to say no.

Allow me to emphasize one last time that it's not my purpose to suggest you adopt any of the following habits. Instead, use this section as a launch pad for your own ideas. It's my hope that the 23 habits profiled below will help you to brainstorm routines that'll make a dramatic and positive difference in your life.

#1 - Eat Breakfast

Most of us grew up hearing this advice. While it's debatable whether breakfast is truly the most important meal of the day, there's no denying its benefits. We enjoy more energy, better focus, and easier weight control (to name just a few).

The problem is, the busyness of our lives often dissuades us from setting aside 15 minutes to enjoy breakfast. Our mornings are rushed and the first meal of the day is usually a casualty of our hectic schedules.

Get into the habit of eating something nutritious in the morning, even if doing so entails waking up 15 minutes earlier.

How to start small: eat an orange, apple, or banana each morning during the first week. These foods require minimal preparation. Graduate to cooked eggs during the second week. Add a slice of toast during the third week. (Note: make adjustments according to personal food intolerances or sensitivities.)

#2 - Practice Active Listening

This is a great habit to develop if you value interpersonal and communication skills. It can strengthen the relationships you share with the people in your life. It can also make you a more effective leader at your job.

Active listening is simply focusing on what a person is saying. Rather than letting our minds wander or thinking of a suitable response, we listen intently to the other person's message. Doing so ensures we interpret it correctly.

How to start small: practice active listening during short, unimportant conversations for the first two weeks. These include conversations you enjoy with strangers. They're likely to be comprised of small talk, so you'll suffer few consequences for letting details slip by you.

During the third and fourth weeks, practice with people whom you see often, but aren't necessarily an important part of your life. Examples include the baristas at your local coffee shop and the clerks at your favorite grocery story.

Practice active listening with your friends and loved ones starting with the fifth week. These conversations are likely to be more intimate with a greater level of trust.

#3 - Do Pushups, Crunches, And Squats

You know that exercise is important. It plays a major role in maintaining good health. Unfortunately, it's one of the first activities we placed on the back burner when our lives become hectic or we feel tired.

But it's easy to develop an exercise habit that sticks.

How to start small: first, put exercise on your daily calendar or to-do list. Schedule it so that it follows a reliable trigger.

Next, choose one form of exercise and decide on a small number of repetitions. For example, you might choose pushups and decide to start with five.

Then, create a schedule that shows how you'll increase the habit over time. When I first began doing pushups, I increased the number of reps by one per week. It worked for me. Do likewise with whatever type of exercise you choose to pursue.

#4 - Master The Art Of Conversation

Making conversation is an art that takes time and effort to master. It's not a matter of saying whatever comes to mind. Rather, it's the art of delicately moving a conversation forward to the delight and engagement of all parties. It requires active listening, identifying shared interests, and recognizing body language and other cues. It also means avoiding common conversation killers, such as interrupting people and monopolizing the spotlight.

With practice, you can become a conversational ninja.

How to start small: during the first two weeks, focus on curbing mistakes you make during conversations. For example, if you tend to argue, work on restraining this tendency. If you speak too quickly, work on slowing your pace.

During the third week, practice one aspect of maintaining good conversations. An example would be to ask purposeful questions relevant to your conversation partner's experience. Alternatively, focus on maintaining an equitable split in how much each party contributes to the conversation.

Practice one additional aspect each week to gradually build your skill set.

#5 - Drink More Water

Most of us don't drink enough water. It's not that we dislike it. We simply don't think about it, or prefer other beverages (soda, coffee, etc.).

But there are many benefits to increasing our water consumption. It improves our digestion, kidney function, and mood. It aids our immune systems and helps to keep fatigue at bay. Drinking more water can also help us control our weight.

If you're not drinking enough, think about how you can increase the amount you consume each day.

How to start small: commit to drinking a small glass of water immediately upon waking in the morning. If you take afternoon naps, do likewise.

Also, keep a small water bottle with you at all times. The ones available in bulk at grocery stores usually hold 17.5

ounces. Commit to drinking half a bottle each day during Week 1. Advance to drinking a full bottle each day during Week 2. Continue to add half a bottle - approximately 9 ounces - each subsequent week for the next few weeks.

Buy a larger water bottle - there are many good options available for less than $20 at Amazon - as your consumption increases. I bought my 24-ounce Contigo bottle for $12.

#6 - Write In A Personal Journal

A lot of people swear by journal writing. They claim it helps them to brainstorm ideas, flesh out complex concepts, and boost their self-discipline. Some claim it plays a key role in helping them to achieve their goals.

Countless historical figures of impressive repute kept personal journals. They include Albert Einstein, Mark Twain, Thomas Edison, Herman Melville, Thomas Jefferson, Leonardo da Vinci, George S. Patton, and Charles Darwin. It's tempting to keep a personal journal, if only to follow in their footsteps. The question is, how do you start if writing doesn't come easy to you?

By starting small, of course!

How to start small: Write 50 words each day for the first week. Increase your output to 100 words per day during Week 2. Continue to increase the number of words you write by 50 per day with the start of each new week.

Within a few months, the habit will be ingrained and you'll be writing daily entries with little internal resistance.

#7 - Compliment Strangers

Everyone loves to receive compliments. But few people take the same pleasure in giving them to others.

It's a good habit to develop, if only for selfish reasons. Complimenting strangers will make you seem more engaging, help you to create trust, and improve your outlook on life. And the best part? It won't cost you a penny.

Adopting this behavior can be difficult for introverts and curmudgeons. Take it slowly and increase it with time.

How to start small: spend two weeks paying one compliment per day to strangers. Be sincere. Don't claim to love the individual's shoes if you think they're ugly.

During Weeks 3 and 4, give two compliments per day.

Starting with Week 5, increase the daily number to three, and include friends and family members.

Do this in person. Paying compliments by text, phone, or email doesn't count.

#8 - Take Short Walks

Everyone loves to take walks. Doing so gives us a chance to get off our backsides and enjoy the fresh air. It's also a great form of low-impact exercise; even though you're unlikely to build up a sweat, you're still moving your body.

The challenge is making the time to take walks. Even short ones. Most of us get so involved with our daily responsibilities that we shelve walks in favor of tasks we consider to be more urgent.

But consider this: taking short daily walks will improve your metabolism, reduce your stress, and help you to control your weight. It can even keep osteoporosis at bay. With those benefits at stake, now may be the time to adopt this habit. Here's how:

How to start small: commit to taking two 5-minute walks each day during the first week. Increase the duration of each walk to 10 minutes starting in Week 2.

In Week 3, maintain the same duration, but increase the number of daily walks to three. Beginning in Week 4, increase the duration of each walk to 15 minutes.

Start taking four walks per day in Week 5. By then, you'll be walking one hour a day. That's more exercise than most people get!

#9 - Read Non-Fiction Books

Reading non-fiction is a completely different experience than reading fiction. Neither is superior to the other. Just different.

Non-fiction exposes us to new ideas and concepts.

In the form of autobiographies and memoirs, it gives us a glimpse into the lives of those who went before us. In the form of essays, it exposes us to others' observations and reasoning. In the form of science journals, it introduces us to a variety of unfamiliar disciplines, from biology to zoology.

Reading non-fiction is more than just a matter of accumulating facts. It's digging deep into subject matter that fascinates us with the hope of learning new things.

If you're not accustomed to reading non-fiction books, it can be difficult to start. It's a tough habit to develop.

For that reason, it's important to start small.

How to start small: read five minutes per day during the first week. Increase the time to 10 minutes per day during the second week.

Starting with Week 3, read 10 minutes per day in the morning and 10 minutes per day in the evening. In Week 4, increase the duration of each reading session to 15 minutes per day. By Week 4, you'll be reading - and hopefully enjoying! - one half-hour of non-fiction reading each day.

#10 - Declutter Your Workspace

I'm certain you already know the benefits of a clean desk. Even if the surface of your desk hasn't seen sunlight for years, you know intuitively that a clean desk is an asset. It improves your ability to concentrate; it makes you less susceptible to distractions; it lowers your stress levels and makes you feel more relaxed. And of course, you'll spend less time looking for things.

So if your desk is a mess, you may be wondering about the best way to get rid of the clutter. Some folks recommend planning a comprehensive declutter initiative, and advise setting aside a few hours to see it through to completion.

As you can probably guess, I recommend the opposite approach.

How to start small: commit to discarding or putting away one item per day during the first two weeks. That's it. No more.

Starting in Week 3, discard or put away two items per day. In Week 4, increase the number to three per day.

Beginning in Week 5, discard or put away one item each time you get up from your desk. Assuming you take occasional breaks, this will ensure several errant items are addressed each day.

The reason I encourage this approach is because it builds a routine. Rather than getting rid of all clutter in a 3-hour window, you develop the decluttering *habit*. Consequently, you're more likely to *keep* your desk clean over the long run.

#11 - Smile At People

Smiling comes naturally to some of us. We smile at everyone we meet, friend or stranger. Others among us are more hesitant. They smile only when the occasion warrants it.

But what if smiling posed health benefits? Wouldn't you make an effort to do it more often?

Scientific research shows that smiling can reduce stress, which, in turn, helps the heart. This causal effect was demonstrated in a study published in the journal *Psychological Science* in 2012.

Let's suppose you want to develop the habit. Here's how to do it...

How to start small: smile at one (extra) person each day for the first week. Focus on strangers and acquaintances. For example, smile at the people you meet while waiting in line at Starbucks. Smile at the checkout clerk at your grocery story.

Each subsequent week, increase the number of people you smile at by one. By the end of the third month, you'll have a reputation as one of the friendliest people in your city.

#12 - Meditate

Meditation has been known to lower stress levels, reduce pain, and lessen anxiety. People who practice it on a regular basis also report that they're able to sleep better, they're more mindful, and feel more relaxed. Some even claim meditation has helped them to beat depression.

In short, there are a lot of reasons to give it a try. The question is, how do you start?

How to start small: the biggest obstacle most people face when they attempt to meditate is sitting still for an extended period. They become restless.

Start by sitting quietly for 60 seconds. Focus on your breathing and being present in the moment. Do this each day for the first week.

Increase the session time to two minutes during Week 2 and three minutes during Week 3.

Lengthen the sessions by one minute each week. Set 10 minutes as your goal. That's plenty of time to enjoy the health benefits associated with meditation.

#13 - Wake Up Earlier

I'm an early riser. Getting up early in the morning allows me to get more things done. I can work in solitude without concern about the phone, unexpected visits from friends and family, or any of the myriad distractions that might disrupt my momentum.

Maintaining a high level of productivity is important to me. I'll bet it's important to you, too. Waking up early is one of the easiest ways to do it. I encourage you to give it a try.

How to start small: set your alarm clock to go off five minutes earlier than normal. Do this each morning during the first week.

During Week 2, set your alarm back another five minutes. During Week 3, set it back yet another five minutes.

At this point, you're getting up 15 minutes earlier. That's not a bad start. Continue setting your alarm clock back five minutes each week. Within three months, you'll be waking up an hour earlier. Because you'll have been working in tiny 5-minute increments, you won't feel as if you've been hit by an 18-wheeler.

#14 - Express Your Gratitude

You've probably heard the phrase "adopt an attitude of gratitude." I used to chuckle when I heard it because it seemed flighty to me. But I've since learned there's a lot to gain by expressing thanks on a regular basis.

Doing so affects my mood and outlook on life. It relaxes me, makes me more optimistic, and keeps my stress levels in check. Expressing gratitude makes me feel better, which probably has a positive effect on my health.

It didn't come naturally to me. I had to build the habit. If you're interested in doing the same, here's the approach I recommend...

How to start small: write down three things for which you're thankful. Do this at the beginning of each day for one week.

During Week 2, continue writing down three items each day, but also express gratitude to one person. You can do it in person, in an email, or with a text. It's up to you. The key is that you do it daily.

Starting in Week 3, increase the number of written items to five. Continue to express your gratitude to one person per day.

Pick a day of the week - for example, Sunday - to review your written notes. You'll have a list of 35 positive items to reflect upon. Imagine how that can affect your mood!

#15 - Keep In Touch With Friends

Our friends improve our lives. They form a support network we can lean on during difficult times. They also serve as a cheering squad when we experience success. Spending time with friends makes us feel more connected, which gives us a sense of satisfaction.

The problem is, we live busy lives. Between our responsibilities at home and the workplace, it's often difficult to keep the connections alive. We tell ourselves that we should call our friends and schedule a dinner date, but the call is never made and the date is never scheduled.

It's a challenge most of us face.

The good news is that it's easy to keep in touch with friends once you build the habit. How do you do that? Try the following…

How to start small: commit to sending one email per week to a friend. Select a day and put the task on your calendar. Make it a recurring item. Do this for eight weeks, reaching out to different friends each week.

Beginning with Week 9, send two emails per week. At this point, you'll be connecting with eight friends per month. You'll hopefully have an opportunity to see them in person along the way.

I recommend sending an email instead of a text. It's more personal, communicates a greater sense of interest, and allows for better expression of your thoughts.

#16 - Help People

Showing kindness to others benefits you as well as them. Think back to the last time you helped someone who was in a jam. Didn't helping them make you feel good? Science says that's a natural side effect of making someone's day. We *feel* good when we *do* good.

If you're unaccustomed to going out of your way to help people, try building the habit. You may be surprised by how good it makes you feel about yourself and the world around you.

Here's how I would approach it…

How to start small: write down a list of the many ways you can help someone. Your list might include things like donating items to charity, babysitting a friend's child, walking a neighbor's dog, or teaching someone a new skill. There are countless ways to show kindness, whether to a friend or stranger. With this list in hand, you'll never be at a loss for ways to help others.

Next, commit to helping one person each day. Offering to help needn't take a lot of time or effort. For example, pick up a neighbor's newspapers if several have accumulated on his or her driveway. Offer to pay for the drink of the person standing behind you at Starbucks.

You don't have to increase the number of people you help each day. Indeed, if you were to do so, you could potentially spend all day helping others to the detriment of your own productivity. If you decide to pursue this habit, its development is more important than the volume of people you help.

#17 - Track How You Spend Your Time

Have you ever felt as if time were slipping between your fingers? You start each day with the hope of getting a lot done only to end the day frustrated. Worse, unless you're tracking your time, it's likely unclear how you spent it. That makes it difficult, even impossible, to make improvements.

I've a big believer in tracking how I use my time each day. I know from firsthand experience that I waste a lot of it if I don't track it. My productivity plummets.

If you've never tracked your time usage, give it a try. You might find that you're wasting time that could otherwise be used to move projects forward, build your business, or hang out with your family.

Getting into the habit isn't difficult. But it does require consistent action. That's where most people stumble. Here's the approach I recommend...

How to start small: create an account at Toggl.com (it's free). Track your time usage for one day. If you spend five minutes checking Facebook, make a note of it. If you take a 15-minute walk, track it. If you work for two hours without a break, record it.

At the end of the day, review how you spent your time. Note where you can tighten things up. For example, you might discover that you spent 12 5-minute sessions on Facebook, Twitter, and Instagram. That's an hour. You may decide to cut that time in half going forward.

Once you've reviewed your first day and made adjustments, track a second day. Then, review it. Look for areas that still warrant adjustments.

Continue doing this until you're comfortable with how you use your time.

Once you're comfortable, conduct weekly reviews to make sure your time usage stays on track.

#18 - Learn New Things

Learning new things makes us more interesting to others. We become better conversationalists when we can intelligently discuss a broader variety of topics.

It also keeps boredom at bay. The brain thrives on new ideas, concepts, and facts. It tries to make connections between what it knows and new things it learns.

You'll also find that learning new things exposes you to people with whom you might not otherwise interact. I've enjoyed many conversations with strangers on a diverse assortment of topics. Some of these strangers have become friends.

How do develop the habit of learning new things? As you might imagine, I recommend starting small.

How to start small: make a list of websites that publish articles on a wide breadth of topics. Examples include MentalFloss.com, TheAtlantic.com, Mashable.com, and Priceonomics.com. Visit one site per day and read a short article. Do this every day for one month.

Keep a list of the new things you learn. Review it at the end of the month. You'll be floored by the range of material you read about. Imagine what you'll learn during the course of one year simply by reading one short article per day!

#19 - Save Money

You already know the many reasons to save money. Doing so helps to fund your retirement. It also ensures you have financial resources to deal with life's curve balls (for example, the urgent need for a new roof on your house). Saving money also helps you to set aside funds for short-term uses. For example, you might want to take a family vacation, start a business, or buy that 98-inch 4K ultra HD 3D LED TV you've been drooling over.

Many people have trouble saving money. It's not because they're struggling to make ends meet. Rather, putting aside money each month is a difficult habit to develop when spending it offers the promise of instant gratification.

So, how do you get into the habit of saving? By starting small, of course!

How to start small: open a savings account and set aside $10 from each paycheck. If you get paid every two weeks, do this for two months. If you get paid on a monthly basis, do this for four months.

When this initial period ends, increase the amount you set aside from each paycheck to $20. Do so for two months (or four monthly if you're paid monthly). Then, increase the amount to $30.

You may be thinking, "At this rate, it'll take me five years to save enough money to take my family on a vacation!" But the point is to develop the saving *habit*. Once the habit has taken root, you can confidently increase the amount you save each month to a figure that supports your goals. At that point, the habit will have become deeply ingrained, making it easier to be consistent.

#20 - Use The Time Chunking Method

The time chunking method is a time management and productivity-boosting strategy. It involves organizing your day into several small chunks of time, and assigning these chunks to specific tasks.

For example, you might spend 30 minutes writing a blog post, 20 minutes reading and responding to emails, and 45 minutes returning phone calls. Each activity would get its own chunk of time. You would ideally schedule short breaks between each chunk to give your brain a rest.

This strategy makes you less vulnerable to distractions and more likely to work in a flow state. I use it myself and have seen my productivity go through the roof.

The challenge is in making the time chunking method a part of your day. It doesn't come naturally to most people. But it can be learned and made a habit with consistent execution. If you're interested in adopting the time chunking method as a part of your day, here's the approach I'd take...

How to start small: create a list of tasks you intend to work on during the current week. Refer to your daily or weekly calendar if you keep one. Or refer to your to-do lists.

During the first week, assign two short (e.g. 30 minutes or less) time chunks to two specific tasks each day.

Starting in Week 2, add a third time chunk and assign its corresponding task. Add a fourth in Week 3 and a fifth in Week 4. Continue adding time chunks, one additional one per week, until your entire day is broken up.

This progression will allow you to grow accustomed to segmenting your day and working in the absence of distractions. Within two months, the habit will have taken root and you'll see a noticeable effect on your productivity.

#21 - Start Each Day With A To-Do List

I'm a huge advocate of using to-do lists as a guide in how I spend my time each day. Many people use to-do lists in some form, even if it entails the use of a single long list of tasks. (I recommend a more comprehensive to-do list system that encourages the use of multiple lists. This system takes context and other factors into account.)

A common mistake is to create such lists in response to a busy day. For example, an individual might arrive at the office and realize he or she has a large number of tasks to address. This person immediately creates a to-do list that details every task.

There's a much better approach: create your to-do list the night before. When you wake up the following morning, you'll know exactly what you need to accomplish. There won't be a sense of urgent desperation.

Here's how I would develop this habit...

How to start small: create a daily to-do list with a maximum of three items. Do so each night before you go to bed for one week. The following day, focus on completing all three tasks on your daily list.

Starting with Week 2, increase the number of items on your daily list to four. Again, create your lists before you go to bed each night. Then, commit to crossing each task off your list the next day.

In Week 3, increase the number of items on your to-do lists to five. As before, create your lists the night before and dedicate yourself to addressing every task the following day.

Continue creating lists with five tasks a day for five more weeks. After eight weeks of daily application, you'll have developed the habit of using to-do lists as well as the habit of creating them before you go to bed. The routine will have become second-nature.

#22 - Learn To Breathe Properly

While breathing takes no effort at all, *proper* breathing takes considerable effort. It entails taking deep breaths - the practice is sometimes called diaphragmatic breathing - rather than the short, shallow gulps of air most of us take by habit.

Why practice deep breathing? Health experts claim it helps us to relax, release tension, and reduce our stress levels. It also improves the delivery of oxygen throughout our bodies, including to our brains. Some people claim it helps them to manage pain and even relieves emotional anxiety.

The good news is that learning to breathe properly is easy, simple, and requires virtually no investment of time. It's just a matter of doing it on a regular basis. Here's how I would develop this habit...

How to start small: During the first week, practice deep breathing while walking. Do this on short walks that you take during breaks. Or do it while walking from your car to the office, the grocery store, or coffee shop. The first week is about looking for opportunities to practice your breathing, not about doing it for a specific period of time.

Starting in Week 2, set aside three minutes in the morning

to practice breathing. Do nothing else. Don't multi-task. Simply close your eyes, relax, and breathe.

Put this activity on your daily calendar or to-do list.

In Week 3, focus on breathing deeply while sitting at your desk. Do this in addition to the three minutes you spend in the morning and any time you spend walking. A few minutes per day should suffice.

At this point, the habit will have begun to take root. You'll have spent three weeks consciously taking deep breaths. But more work remains. Most people find they need to remind themselves to breathe properly, even after months of conscious practice.

#23 - Take Immediate Action

Many people have difficulty taking action. Reasons vary. Some folks fear failure. Others are disinclined to try new things. Still others are saddled with indecision to the point that they become paralyzed when confronted with multiple options.

But making decisions and acting on them quickly can benefit you in several ways. First, you become more committed to the path you choose for yourself. Second, you radiate confidence, an essential trait if you serve in a leadership role. Third, it improves communication; others will realize you're disinclined to vacillate and respond in a similar manner. Fourth, you accomplish more.

These advantages are tough to ignore. If you tend to dither when making decisions and forging ahead, consider developing this habit. It can literally change your life.

If you're unaccustomed to taking immediate action, here's how I would build this habit...

How to start small: Compile a list of tasks you've put on the back burner. During Week 1, pick one task from the list each day. Regardless of the reason you put it off (procrastination, a fear of failure, etc.), commit to finishing it before the end of the day.

Beginning in Week 2, continue to work through your list of postponed tasks, addressing one per day. In addition, spend 10 minutes per day cleaning up your email inbox. This is a common area of indecision for people. Train yourself to deal with each email decisively. Respond to it, delete it, or archive it.

During Week 3, focus on making at least one decision quickly per day. When confronted with multiple options, choose one within 10 seconds. For example, let's say your spouse asks you which restaurant you'd like to visit for dinner. Instead of spending five minutes considering every local venue, just choose one. Be decisive.

Starting in Week 4, look for opportunities to make quick decisions and take immediate action.

For example, if you're presented with more than one set of driving directions, pick one and move on. If you're at the grocery store and trying to decide between chocolate chip ice cream or Rocky road, choose one and put it in your shopping cart. If you're trying to decide between two wines for a dinner party, make a fast decision. Give yourself 10 seconds.

* * *

As I noted at the beginning of this section, these 23 habits are merely ideas. They're designed to help you brainstorm routines that will improve your daily experience.

Experiment with them. Or let them provide a spark of creativity and inspiration that leads you to other habits that might have an even greater impact on your quality of life.

If they manage to serve that purpose, they'll have done their job.

Final Thoughts On Using Small Habits To Transform Your Life

You now have everything you need to form good habits that stick. You're familiar with cues, routines, and rewards, and the part each plays in developing long-term behavioral patterns. You also have several tools and tactics at your disposal for making sure your new habits last the test of time.

The only ingredient left in this recipe for success is your willingness to apply what you've learned. The good news is that applying the proven 10-step system for habit development I've described is easy.

Remember, the core theme of *Small Habits Revolution* is to develop new habits by starting with tiny routines that cause zero discomfort. These routines are small enough that they make it difficult to say no. With time, increase each habit according to your desired outcome. They'll gradually become so entrenched that they stick for years to come.

If you're looking for a way to transform your life, start small. In a couple years, when you look back to monitor your progress, you'll realize the small steps you took turned into great strides toward a more rewarding life!

Did You Enjoy Reading *Small Habits Revolution?*

Thank you so much for investing in this action guide and reading it through to the end. That means more to me than I can express. It's my hope that the information in *Small Habits Revolution* will help you to adopt good habits that'll enrich your life.

I realize there are many books available on habit development. I'm honored and flattered that you chose to read this one.

May I ask you a small favor? Would you take a moment to leave a review for *Small Habits Revolution* at Amazon? Your thoughts will help other people decide if my book will help them to achieve the results they desire.

If you'd like to receive early notification when I release a new action guide (at a steep discount), be sure to join my mailing list at http://artofproductivity.com/free-gift/. You'll receive my 40-page Special Report *Catapult Your Productivity: The Top 10 Habits You Must Develop To Get More Things Done* (PDF). You'll also receive periodic tips, tricks, and hacks for managing your time, increasing your daily productivity, and designing a more rewarding lifestyle.

All the best,
Damon Zahariades
http://artofproductivity.com

About The Author

Damon Zahariades is a corporate refugee who endured years of unnecessary meetings, drive-by chats with coworkers, and a distraction-laden work environment before striking out on his own. Today, in addition to being the author of a growing catalog of time management and productivity books, he's the showrunner for the productivity blog ArtofProductivity.com.

In his spare time, he shows off his copywriting chops by powering the content marketing campaigns used by today's growing businesses to attract customers.

Damon lives in Southern California with his beautiful, supportive wife and their frisky dog. He's currently staring down the barrel of his 50th birthday.

Other Books by Damon Zahariades

Morning Makeover: How To Boost Your Productivity, Explode Your Energy, and Create An Extraordinary Life - One Morning At A Time!

If you win the morning, you win the day. Here's how to create a morning routine that can literally change your life!

* * *

Fast Focus: A Quick-Start Guide To Mastering Your Attention, Ignoring Distractions, And Getting More Done In Less Time!

Are you constantly distracted? Does your mind wander after just a few minutes? Learn how to develop laser-sharp focus!

* * *

To-Do List Formula: A Stress-Free Guide To Creating To-Do Lists That Work!

Finally! A step-by-step system for creating to-do lists that'll actually help you to get things done!

* * *

The 30-Day Productivity Plan: Break The 30 Bad Habits That Are Sabotaging Your Time Management - One Day At A Time!

Need a daily action plan to boost your productivity? This 30-day guide is the solution to your time management woes!

* * *

The Time Chunking Method: A 10-Step Action Plan For Increasing Your Productivity

It's one of the most popular time management strategies used today. Double your productivity with this easy 10-step system.

* * *

Digital Detox: Unplug To Reclaim Your Life

Addicted to technology? Here's how to disconnect and enjoy real, meaningful connections that lead to long-term happiness.

* * *

Small Habits Revolution: 10 Steps To Transforming Your Life Through The Power Of Mini Habits!

Got 5 minutes a day? Use this simple, effective plan for creating any new habit you desire!

* * *

For a complete list, please visit
http://artofproductivity.com/my-books/